Messenger of Love and Peace
St. Pio of Pietrelcina

A Children's Biography

By

Elvira Mucciarone Janz

**James F. Lincoln
Library**

Lake Erie College
**Painesville, OH
44077**

ISBN: 1-4033-3842-6 (e-book)
ISBN: 1-4033-3843-4 (Paperback)
ISBN: 1-4033-3844-2 (Hardcover)

This book is printed on acid free paper.

1stBooks - rev. 10/15/02

Cover Picture of St. Pio courtesy of

Edizioni "Voce di Padre Pio"

DEDICATION

This book is dedicated to my three children,

Eric, Brian and Carla

ACKNOWLEDGEMENTS

My book would not have been written without the assistance of so many people. Researching information for a book is not only time consuming but also one must be careful that all information is documented. It has taken four years to research and write the book. I wrote my book about St. Pio of Pietrelcino because I wanted children all over the world to know about this wonderful saint. St. Pio had great love and respect for children. Many children received blessings and miracles from the stigmatist of San Giovanni Rotondo. St. Pio's prayers never stopped.

I wish to thank Father Gerardo Di Flumeri, Vice - Postulate of the Capuchin Fathers of Our Lady of Grace Friary, San Giovanni Rotondo, Italy. His permission to use pictures and information of St. Pio is appreciated. The comments Father Di Flumeri wrote for my books were most encouraging. I wish to acknowledge Mr. and Mrs. Hafer and son, Jacob, of Pennsylvania for the account of his miracle. I communicated with the Hafer's by phone interviews and letters. I am grateful to Paul Walsh and his mother, Mrs. Walsh, for permission to use the miracle that Paul received from St. Pio. Their phone interviews and precious letters will not be forgotten.

I would like to thank Tan Books and Publishers, Inc. for their help. My deepest appreciation goes to Father Schug for the phone communication, written communication (e-mail) and his kind comments written for my book. You are truly a man of God. In addition, I am deeply appreciative to Edmund C. Lane, S.S.P., Society of St. Paul/ALBA HOUSE for permission to use valuable information.

I wish to thank Brother William Fackovec from the University of Dayton and Marian Library, Dayton, Ohio for his kindness and help in my research. The National Centre for Padre Pio in Barto, Pennsylvania is also recognized for their assistance and time. Their valuable information was most helpful. Special thanks to Mrs. Vera Calandra, Maria Calandra and Veramarie Calandra for their continuous support.

I would like to recognize my son Dr. Brian Janz for his help with the medical aspects of my book. His devotion and support during my medical crisis in July 2000 will never be forgotten. My son is specializing in surgery at Harvard Medical School. I send love and gratitude, to my daughter Carla A. Berkshire who encouraged me to write the book. In addition, I would like to thank my son, Eric E. Janz, for his continuous love and protection. To my dearest friends Oscar T., Rustie, Pepper, Little Oscar, Omar, Tyler, Lexi and Casey, may St. Pio of Pietrelcina bless and protect you. To my late beloved grandmother, Elvira Mucciarone, my gratitude and love for all the prayers and songs she taught me as I was growing up. My grandmother's love for St. Pio made quite an impression on me. I would like to thank my parents, Biagio and Addolorata Mucciarone for their love and devotion.

Last but not least, I want to personally thank St. Pio of Pietrelcina for saving my life on July 3, 2000.

Elvira Mucciarone Janz - Author

Padre Pio's love for children has been aptly demonstrated by the numerous miracles obtained from God through his intercession on their behalf. May this book be a source of inspiration for youth to take Padre Pio's holy life as an example to be emulated.

Father Gerardo Di Flumeri
Vice Postulator
San Giovanni Rotondo, Italy

x

INTRODUCTION

I'd like to introduce you to St. Pio of Pietrelcina. I think he is the most gifted saint who ever lived. His most conspicuous gift was the stigmata (say STIG-mah-tah), that is, the five wounds of the crucified Christ - real holes - in his hands, feet, and side, for the last 50 years of his life. He died in 1968, in San Giovanni Rotondo, in southern Italy. I think God gave him these stigmata as God's own "Good Housekeeping Seal of Approval," as if to tell the world: "Here is My man, and here is My proof!" For many, meeting him was the difference between life and death, literally!

John A. Schug, OFM, Capuchin

AUTHOR'S NOTE

Throughout the book Padre Pio is referred to as Francesco, Fra Pio, Padre Pio, Blessed Padre Pio and St. Pio of Pietrelcina. The names refer to the same person.

Up through his teenage years, he was known as Francesco. While attending his religious studies, he came to be known as Fra Pio. When Fra Pio took all of his vows toward the priesthood, he was called Padre Pio. He became Blessed Padre Pio after his beatification on May 2, 1999. The beatification is the last step before sainthood. Once Blessed Padre Pio was canonized and became a saint, his title became St. Pio of Pietrelcina.

Elvira Mucciarone Janz
Author

TABLE OF CONTENTS

CHAPTER 1

Veramarie Calandra was dying. The two-year-old girl had already endured four surgeries. Surgeons had removed her bladder. She was born with irregular urinary tract.

In 1963, someone had given the Calandra's a book on Padre Pio. Mrs. Calandra had read the book and had put it away. During her daughter's health crisis, someone mentioned Padre Pio. Mrs. Calandra looked for the book and found the address to the monastery in Italy. She sent a cable.

A few days later a form letter from Padre Pio arrived in the United States. It said that Mrs. Calandra's intentions would be prayed for. Veramarie showed some improvement.

Later, Mrs. Calandra sent another cable to Padre Pio.

Again, she received a letter. The message was the same as the earlier one. In August of 1968, Mrs. Calandra smelled wonderful fragrance of roses. Shortly after, Mrs. Calandra heard Padre Pio's voice saying, "Do not delay, come immediately."[1]

A week later, Mrs. Calandra arrived at the monastery in Italy with Veramarie and the four weeks infant named Christina. When she arrived at the monastery she was told to come back at 2:30 p.m. in the sacristy. She was told to kneel and not to speak to Padre Pio unless he spoke to her.

Padre Pio came into the sacristy in a wheel chair. He looked tired. The priest stopped and placed his hands on the infant Christina and then on Veramarie. Padre Pio didn't speak to Mrs. Calandra.

The next day she was told to kneel in the corridor for Padre Pio. It was 7:30 in the morning. Padre Pio again placed his hands on both girls. He looked at Mrs. Calandra with his kind and knowing eyes. He held his wounded hand up to Mrs. Calandra. She kissed it.

When she arrived back in the United States, the doctors took x-rays of Veramarie. They told the Calandra's that a small piece of the bladder had shown up on Veramaries's x-rays.

Approximately two weeks later Padre Pio died. Mrs. Calandra knew that Padre Pio had presented her two year-old daughter with a miracle by giving her a new bladder.

Who was Padre Pio from Pietrelcina, Italy? He was born Francesco Forgione and was known as Padre Pio of Pietrelcina for fifty-two years in the Capuchin Order. He was the only priest in the history of the Catholic Church to be stigmatized. He was marked with the religious stigmata. Padre Pio received the five wounds of Jesus on September 20, 1918. He was a miracle worker.

At age five he gave himself forever to God. He had visions of Jesus, the Blessed Mother and his guardian angel, which he loved. He used to call his guardian angel "The companion of my infancy."[2] His guardian angel took the appearance of a young boy. They played and spoke together. Francesco thought he was from the neighborhood!

Francesco also struggled with devils. These evil visits came in hideous shapes of humans and beasts. These uninvited evil visitors not only upset Francesco, but he was afraid of them. Francesco also had to deal with ill health most of his life. He loved God so much that he tried to work through whatever struggle came his way.

Francesco didn't mince his words with others. He spoke his mind. The young boy could be stubborn. He also had a temper when things didn't go his way.

Francesco was quiet and obedient to his parents, but he got himself into creative situations. At age ten he came down with a fever and intestinal infection. Since it was harvest time in southern Italy, Francesco wanted to see his much-loved farmland called Piana Romana. His mother had prepared hot fried peppers as a treat for the farmhands. Francesco asked for some hot peppers but was refused.

He asked his mother to close the bedroom door because he wanted to rest. Soon after, Francesco scooted out of bed and ate the rest of the hot peppers. His mother yelled at his older brother for allowing the dog to get at the food. Finally, Francesco fessed up to who actually ate them.

Once, his Uncle Pelligrino had asked Francesco to go buy some cigars and matches. Coming back home, Francesco gave in to his temptation and took a puff of the cigar. He became sick. The experience cured him of any desire to smoke.

Religion was instilled into Francesco and his siblings at an early age. Francesco always wanted to go to church from the time he could speak.

He was kind and giving. As a young boy he played and enjoyed himself. Francesco liked to wrestle with his friend Luigi Orlando just for fun; however, if any swearing words were said, he would stop the game and walk away. A boyhood friend of Francesco once said that while the rest of the children were naughty, he was always well behaved.

When Francesco was ten, he told his parents he wanted to be a priest of the Capuchin Order. In his youth, it was common for Capuchin friars to come and collect donations. They usually carried a big sack to hold the various foods collected. Fra Camilo of Sant'Elia, Italy had this job in Francesco's town.

Francesco loved this friar. He was kind to everyone. Francesco watched Fra Camilo and listened to his every word. He decided that someday he would enter this order. Francesco was also impressed with the beards that the order was allowed to have. Padre Pio would say years later, "I had gotten the idea of Fra Camillo's beard into my head and no one could take away my desire to be a bearded friar."[3]

His parents were poor farmers, but rich in love, loyalty and devotion for the family and others. Francesco lived in a one-story, two-room stone house with his parents and siblings. Francesco was the second of eight children. Michael was the oldest. Francesco also had sisters named Felicita, Pellegrina and Grazia. Grazia later became a nun. Three of Francesco siblings died in infancy.

Francesco's father, Grazio Forgione, was a peasant farmer and a hard worker. He was kind, religious, had a wonderful singing voice and loved to tell stories. He traveled to Brazil and America to work and save money for Francesco's education as a priest. He ruled the house with an iron fist, but did everything to make a better life for his family. He was proud that his son wanted to become a priest. Francesco didn't always see eye-to-eye with his dad, but he was close to him. His father taught his children that when problems came up, they were to be discussed, solved and to move on. Mr. Forgione was kind to the environment and any living things.

Giuseppa DeNunzio Forgione was Francesco's mother. Her side of the family not only had more land but money. She was religious and instilled in Francesco his love for God and the Blessed Mother at an early age. She took care of her family. She also worked the several parcels of land they owned when her husband was out of the country looking for work. Mrs. Forgione wasn't afraid of hard work. Francesco loved her very much. Both of his parents were a great influence on him.

Francesco loved his siblings, too, and got along fine with them. He deeply cared for his sister Felicita. She was sincere and sweet. He loved to tease Felicita and pull boyish pranks on her. As an adult, Padre Pio would comment on his sister Felicita, calling her a "saint" and "the best in the family."[4]

The central theme in the Forgione's family was love for God and others. Francesco learned what he lived and lived what he learned. His parent's simplicity and love was instilled in Francesco and his siblings at an early age. It would stay with them for the rest of their lives. Francesco learned the direct ways his parents communicated with others.

Pietrelcina, Italy was a rural village of about 5,000 people during Francesco's boyhood. After World War I about 3,000 people remained. Many people emigrated to other countries or different parts of Italy. They wanted a better life for themselves and their families. Pietrelcina was located in a hilly area with view of the mountains.

The stone houses had roofs of hollow tile made from hard clay. The houses were close together and didn't allow much privacy. The homes didn't have central heating in those days. A fireplace was one of the main means of heat. If families were fortunate to have a bed-warmer, it would provide some heating comfort. Coals were placed in the covered pan and positioned between the sheets for a few minutes. The pan would be quickly removed to prevent fire.

Francesco had three years of free public school when he was young. In those days, children had to help their parents with the farm work. School was held in the evening. Francesco did well in this setting, although the first two teachers were private tutors. Once he made up his mind to become a Capuchin priest, further education was needed.

When Francesco was ten, his parents sent him to the Don Tizzani's school. Mr. Tizzani was a former priest. Francesco studied with him for three years. He showed poor progress. It became a great concern for his parents. Francesco thought well of his teacher, but his father felt uncomfortable with Mr. Tizzani's position as an ex-clergyman. Mr. Forgione wrote to his wife from America to place Francesco in another school.

Francesco's mom did exactly that. His mother found a new teacher by the name of Angelo Caccavo. Francesco was attentive to his schoolwork and progressed well. Mr. Caccavo was a strict teacher. He often used a ruler on students if their assignments were not completed.

Some of the boys in class decided to play a practical joke on Francesco. They wrote a love letter and signed his name on it. They passed it to a girl in the classroom who handed it over to Mr. Caccavo. The teacher hit Francesco in front of the class. Francesco tried to protect himself by hiding under the desk! When Mr. Caccavo realized the note was a bad joke, he felt terrible. Francesco resented have been made the scapegoat for his teacher's rage. In those days, hitting students was common. Francesco had black and blue marks that stayed with him for quite a long time. Later in life, Padre Pio was said to have always prayed for Mr. Caccavo.

Francesco was quiet in class. He was not only handsome but also had a beautiful smile. When the girls in his class talked to him, he became shy and lowered his eyes. He respected girls, but kept his distance.

Francesco knew his purpose in life was to be a servant of the Lord. He tried to obey his parents. However, once he made up his mind to do something, he would see it through.

In 1902, a year before he was to enter the monastery of Morcone, Italy, Francesco wanted to go on a field trip to the Blessed Mother of Pompeii with his class. His father was in America working, and Francesco knew his mother wouldn't allow him to go on the trip. Still, he continued with his plans to go. When his father wrote from America and complained about the money his son spent on the trip, Francesco wrote back: "Concerning the complaint to Mother about my going to Pompeii you are right a thousand times. However...next year...all festivals...will be finished because I shall abandon this life and embrace a better one..."[5]

Francesco continued to study and made preparations to enter the novitiate at Morcone, Italy with the help of his Uncle Pelligrino and Father Pannullo, the parish priest of Pietrelcina. When Francesco first applied for admission to the Capuchin Order, it was denied because the student quota for the incoming class had been met. The family tried to persuade Francesco to enter different orders. They were met with a single question from Francesco, "Do they have beards?" When he could not be assured, Francesco responded, "Then I say no."[6]

A few months later, an acceptance letter came from the Capuchin Order. Francesco, however, had another surprise in his path. A classmate delivered a cruel joke in form of a letter about a supposed relationship between Francesco and a girl. Father Pannullo took the letter seriously. He ordered an internal investigation and had Francesco's movements followed. Francesco had no knowledge of this, except that he received a suspension from serving as an altar boy. Francesco thought about the suspension, but went about his work and preparation for the monastery. The result- no wrong doing.

After the investigation, the handwriting on the letter was determined and the accuser was caught. The other young man confessed to writing the letter in order to ruin Francesco's character and reputation. When Francesco found out about the accusation and investigation, he was baffled! Later in life, he was asked if he held any bad feelings toward people who attempted to slander and misdirect his life. He told his superior, "I prayed for those who slandered me and I will continue to pray for them. The most I ever said was an occasional: 'Lord, if a whipping is necessary to convert them, give it to them, but only if it will do them some good' "[7]

Shortly before Francesco was to formally enter his religious studies, he became ill with symptoms of failing energies. The doctor examined him. The tests showed no sign of the tuberculosis they had suspected. The tests showed that Francesco was disposed to bronchial infections, which is a type of lung inflammation. Francesco had bouts of this disease most of his life.

Francesco private life was coming to a close. He loved God with everything he was, but Francesco also loved his parents and siblings.

9

They were a close and loving family who would go above and beyond for each other. Francesco dreaded the coming separation.

In 1903, visions from the Lord gently but firmly prompted Francesco into his new religious life. One day, after Francesco had received Holy Communion in church, he found himself in a big hall. On one side of the hall were normal-looking people, but the other side showed demons with grotesque faces. The blessed Jesus appeared next to Francesco. Shortly after, an enormous monster came into the large room and directed himself toward Francesco. Francesco was terrified. Before the hideous monster could touch him, a bolt of light struck the monster. The monster vanished with a repulsive screech. Then Jesus turned to Francesco and said, "That is the fiend whom you will have to fight."[8] The beautiful vision of our Lord disappeared.

Soon after, Francesco was walking with Father Pannullo and friends when Francesco suddenly stopped. He said, "What a beautiful aroma. I smell incense and hear the chanting of friars."[9] Francesco pointed out the location where the Capuchin monastery and church would be built. Some of Francesco's friends patronized or made fun of his prediction.

In January of 1903, Francesco was ready to leave his home for his new religious life. He tried to be brave. His dad was still in America working, but Francesco had written to his father and had assured him that Michael, the older brother, would take care of the family. Francesco's heart was breaking in separating from his beloved family. He made his personal good-byes to every member of his family.

Finally, he hugged his mother and knelt down to receive her blessing. Mrs. Forgione cried and blessed her son saying, "My dear child, my heart is bleeding, but St. Francis has called you and you must go."[10]

On January 6, 1903, Francesco along with two other young men set forth to Marcone by train. Francesco's Uncle Pellegrino and teacher, Don Angelo Caccavo, went with the boys. When Francesco arrived at the Capuchin monastery in Marcone, his friend and mentor, Fra Camillo met him at the door. The man who had made the greatest impact on Francesco to enter the Capuchin Order was smiling at him. His friend not only welcomed Francesco but also walked him through the door to his new religious life.

CHAPTER 2

The coming months weren't easy for Francesco. He was happy to work toward his dream of becoming a priest, but he missed his family and friends. He was allowed to see members of his family, but only for a short time. The Capuchin Order taught Francesco humility, obedience, purity, self-denial, sacrifices and poverty. He also had to learn to separate himself from the outside world. This included family and friends.

When Francesco's mother visited, however, he wouldn't hug or kiss her. He kept his distance. Later, he would say that when he saw his mother, he had a great desire to embrace her. Due to the rules of the Capuchin Order, he could not.

Life in the monastery was demanding. Francesco didn't have much time for himself. He had to keep up with his studies and learn the various prayers said day and night. Francesco also had to clean areas of the monastery, which included toilets, floors and the kitchen. He didn't get much sleep either. He had to get up for several hours during the night to pray with the other novices. He was up at five o'clock to begin the day. When the superiors allowed an hour off, Francesco had to reflect and open his heart to the Lord. The superiors allowed interactions amongst the novices during free time, but they were encouraged to talk about religious subjects.

Francesco worked hard at his studies, but he also had a great sense of humor. He was loved and respected by his peers and superiors. He enjoyed telling jokes with other novices. Francesco even played pranks! One night, as he was coming out of the bathroom, he saw another young novice. Francesco hid behind a stand and made some rather loud and scary sounds. The second novice, unsure of the noise, walked very fast to his room. Francesco followed him, but the young novice began running even harder. Afraid that he was going to be caught, Francesco ran quickly after his friend. When he finally reached the young novice, they tripped and fell on top of each other!

On January 22, 1903 Francesco was vested in the Capuchin habit. His habit consisted of a hood, belt and scapular. A scapular is a monk's sleeveless outer garment, which hangs from the shoulders. Sometimes a scapular will have a cowl or hood. He also received the tonsure, which was a symbolic haircut of the Capuchin Order. Francesco's short haircut came halfway around his head. He took the name of Frate Pio until he was ordained a priest. Frate means brother as in Brother Pio. He also began growing his beloved beard. He was fifteen years old.

Frate Pio's room at the monastery was small and sparse. It contained a bed, chair, writing desk, washstand, water pitcher and a cross on the wall. He and other novices had to keep their room clean at all times. The novices had to sleep on their backs with their hands in form of a cross. The Capuchin Order believed this would keep away various forms of evils.

In addition to his formal education, he also had group studies with his religious director at the monastery. He didn't have any problems with his studies. He studied every minute he had free. His goal was to become a good priest. However, there wasn't enough time in the day to do everything that he wanted to accomplish. His physical being suffered as a result. He pushed himself to the limit.

The only heat was in the community room. The bedrooms were unheated, even in the coldest of weather. Frate Pio and the other novices were given only a couple of blankets for their room. He and the other novices had to go barefooted. Everyone else wore sandals, but not the novices. This practice didn't help Frate Pio's health.

The food in the monastery was not only meager but also unappealing. In those days, one could not order out pizza or hamburgers. Sparse meals had to be accepted without complaining. One full meal and two smaller ones were offered each day. Many novices had a difficult time adjusting to these modest menus. Frate Pio didn't make a big fuss. He would eat little or no food. Often, his superiors were concerned about his eating habits and encouraged Frate Pio to eat more.

Superiors also revoked privileges without explaining the reasons. Novices had food taken away from them without warning. They also had to kneel from a few minutes to hours at a time. It depended on the level of punishment the superior felt was needed. When a few novices couldn't tolerate these practices, they went home.

Frate Pio didn't complain about these rigid rules. He believed in self-discipline and denials. However, his conscientious efforts affected his physical health. Frate Pio experienced mysterious high fevers that would break bathroom thermometers. The thermometers were made from glass and mercury. After a short time, the high fevers would disappear.

Shortly after Frate Pio's dad came back from America in 1903, he went to see his son at the monastery. Mr. Forgione was shocked and upset by his son's weak condition. Frate Pio kept his head down and hands folded when he saw his father. He didn't say anything. Mr. Forgione went to the superior and demanded to know what had happened to his son. The superior tried to assure Mr. Forgione, but the distressed father wasn't satisfied. He wanted to take his son home, but the Capuchin Order wouldn't allow this. His parents stayed with him for several days before going home.

Frate Pio's health kept deteriorating as the year went on. His superiors made a decision.

As a result, he returned home when he became too ill to stay at the monastery. He was very much missed when he temporarily left his religious family. Everyone enjoyed his company. His religious family was touched by his love for prayers and humble ways. People were drawn to him through his gentle demeanors. Frate Pio's understanding and love came from deep within him.

In 1904, Frate Pio took his temporary vows toward his priesthood. Frate Pio would live for three years in poverty, chastity and obedience. These rules were in accordance with the teachings of St. Francis for the Capuchin students.

Seminary schools or colleges were not available during Fra Pio's student days. He had to travel to various friaries or monasteries for his education toward the priesthood. It meant adjusting to new places and people. Frate Pio adjusted to the various environments, but his health became worse. His high fevers continued along with weakness and lack of appetite.

Between January 1904 to 1910, Frate Pio traveled to about six monasteries for his education. In 1907, he took his permanent or solemn vows toward the priesthood.

During Frate Pio's studies at the monastery of Serracapriola, Italy, Padre Agostino and Padre Benedette were two of his professors. Both were to influence Frate Pio's life for many years.

Frate Pio's study for the priesthood continued to be marred by problems the devil caused him. The devil would appear to him in different ways. The devil did everything to annoy and trick Frate Pio. The devil would appear as monks, dogs, men, boys, and ugly images. Frate Pio continued to be shocked and frightened by these appearances. They took his energy away. He would deal with these terrible visits all his life. There was no way out.

One sultry summer night, Frate Pio couldn't sleep. He heard movements in the next room. He went to the window and spoke to his friend. What Frate Pio saw next horrified him. An ugly, giant black dog sat on the windowsill and stared at him with wild eyes. Before

Frate Pio could react, the savage looking dog bounced and disappeared over the top of the building. Later, Frate Pio found out that the brother living next door had moved out earlier that evening. The room had been empty.

Often, demons came to his room and dared Frate Pio to fight with them. They also made fun of him. One time, an ugly demon was disguised as Frate Pio's superior. The devil told Frate Pio to change his religious ways. The fiend said that the Lord didn't care for his devotions. Frate Pio became suspicious. He repeated the name of Jesus. At once, the grotesque shape disappeared. The only reminder was a sulfurous or rotten egg smell.

Other times, Frate Pio would come back from classes or work duties and find his cell in a mess. His belongings would be thrown all over. He would have to clean up everything. The devil threw ink on his school materials. His guardian angel would come to his aide by allowing Frate Pio to read or decipher the ink-stained areas. The guardian angel would also help retrieve the papers that were thrown all over.

After the visits by the devil, Jesus and the Blessed Mother would also come to comfort him. He not only saw but also spoke to Jesus and the Blessed Mother. They assured him of their love and protection. Frate Pio called the Blessed Mother, "Little Mother."[1]

The many visits that Frate Pio received from Jesus, the Blessed Mother and his guardian angel gave him the renewed strength to go on. He was chosen by God to be one with Him and bring people to the Lord. His main goal was to glorify God through prayers, work and deeds.

Frate Pio was ordained a Capuchin priest on August 10, 1910 in the cathedral of Benevento, Italy. He was twenty-three years old. From this point, he was called Padre Pio. His mother and siblings attended the ordination. Padre Pio's dad and brother were working in Jamaica, New York and couldn't attend his ordination.

His mother, Mrs. Forgione, honored him with a huge party with delicious food, such as rigatoni or spaghetti, roasted chickens, sausages; salted ham called prosciuto, cheeses of various type, fruits and desserts. The town's band played beautiful Italian music for the occasion. Everyone had a good time.

Padre Pio was honored by the celebration, but kept his head down and appeared shy. Padre Pio would refer to the day he became a priest as, "That beautiful day of my ordination."[2]

Padre Pio never wanted to be the center of attention. He did everything possible to avoid fame and attention. His goal was to do God's work. However, despite his purity of heart and humble attitudes, fame found Padre Pio.

CHAPTER 3

From 1909 to 1916, Padre Pio often returned to his hometown of Pietrelcina for health reasons. He was plagued with intestinal problems, vomiting, strong coughs and headaches. This saddened Padre Pio because he loved his religious life and wanted to stay there.

His superiors tried everything. They send Padre Pio to monasteries where the air was fresh and clear. The Capuchin Order even made sure doctors examined him. Finally, they sent him home to heal and recover.

As soon as he went to Pietrelcina, Padre Pio would feel somewhat better. The fresh air of his hometown agreed with him. His parents, though, insisted on taking him to be examined by specialists. Mr. and Mrs. Forgione paid those medical bills from their own pockets. Padre Pio didn't feel his parents should pay for his medical expenses. He wrote letters to his superior expressing his views.

Mr. and Mrs. Forgione were happy and proud that their son was a Capuchin priest, but they worried about his health. Mrs. Forgione didn't want her son to go back to the monastery. She tried to talk Padre Pio in staying in Pietrelcina. Padre Pio wouldn't hear of this! These differences caused a conflict between mother and son.

Padre Pio stayed in the tower or at Pianna Romana when he came home to rest and recuperate. The tower was part of the Forgione's house. Pianna Romana was where the Forgione family worked their parcels of land. Padre Pio's dad had fixed up the cabin for his son's use.

On September 7,1910, Padre Pio was praying in the one-room cabin in Pianna Romana. During prayer time, he noticed wounds in the middle of his hands. He didn't know what to make of the lesions. He confided in his friend, archpriest Don Pannullo. Afterwards, Padre Pio saw several doctors about his medical condition. No conclusive diagnosis was made. Each doctor had his own medical explanation.

Padre Pio had received a form of the visible stigmata from Jesus at his beloved Pianna Romana! No medical knowledge could explain this phenomenal or fabulous wonder.

Padre Pio wanted to suffer alone for the glory of God. He didn't want anyone to know about the sores on his hands. He was embarrassed and confused by the lesions. He wanted them to go away! So, feeling depressed, he went back to archpriest Pannullo.

Together they prayed that Jesus would remove them. The wounds disappeared, but the pain in his hands remained. Padre Pio had to deal with the pain and discomfort for quite a while.

Finally, in 1911, Padre Pio confided to his superior, Padre Benedetto. The wounds had appeared again. He felt such shame.

In a letter to Padre Benedetto on September 8, 1911, Padre Pio wrote: "Yesterday evening something happened...In the center of the palms of my hands a red patch appeared about the size of a centesimo [penny]…The pain was more acute in the left hand…I also feel some pain in the soles of my feet."[1]

Other researchers have called this event the Invisible Stigmata, but Padre Pio's letter to his spiritual director said otherwise.

As he furthered his relationship with God, Padre Pio offered himself as a victim for others. He wrote to his superior, "For some time I have felt the need to offer myself to the Lord as victim for poor sinners and for the souls in Purgatory."[2]

Padre Benedetto wanted him to come back to the religious community. Padre Pio was uncertain about his return. He wrote a testy letter to his superior about his feelings. He missed the community life, but didn't want to return and become ill all over again. In Pietrelcina, he could at least say mass, but was afraid that once he entered the monastery, his health problems would make that impossible.

Padre Benedetto took offense to his letter and wrote back: "…I hope that this will be the last time that you refuse to submit to my instruction. Otherwise, I shall not write to you anymore. You have hurt me by telling me that my love is finite since I want to cause your death."[3] Return Padre Pio did, but not for long. Shortly after he re-entered the monastery, he became ill with stomach problems and vomiting. He couldn't hold down any form of food or liquid.

During this short stay at the friary, Padre Pio had many visions from Jesus. He also received a visit from St. Francis. Padre Pio was afraid that he would be asked to leave the priesthood due to his continuous health problems. In fact, this possibility had been discussed by the Capuchin Order. In a vision, St. Francis assured the young priest that he wouldn't be kicked out of the Capuchin Order. St. Francis relayed Jesus's message to Padre Pio. He was to go back to Pietrelcina!

Padre Pio's illness over-took him even more. He had fevers with great amount of sweating, pains in the chest area and rheumatic pains in his entire body. In December of 1911, he returned home to Pietrelcina.

The road back to his city was to prepare for his long ministry.

The Lord was laying the groundwork for Padre Pio's holiness. The next five years were hard on Padre Pio. He felt alone and isolated from the Capuchin Order, his hometown and at times even his family. Padre Pio wished his health were better so he could participate in the Capuchin community life. This was not to be. He knew that the Lord meant for him to stay in Pietrelcina for an extended time.

Padre Pio also returned home because of problems his sister was causing for herself and the family. In later years, he told his niece that he was needed at home.

Padre Pio's mother wanted her son to regain his health. She continued to beg Padre Pio to put in a request to the Capuchin Order to become a parish priest. She felt that the Capuchin Order was placing too many demands on him. Her pleading had become more insistent. Mrs. Forgione had even asked Father Pannullo to join forces with her.

Her strong concerns placed undo stress on Padre Pio's health. He would not comply with her wishes. This added to the hurt and resentment between mother and son. In a letter to Padre Agostino in 1912, Padre Pio said, "In my greatest sufferings it seems to me that I no longer have a mother on this earth, but a very compassionate one in heaven."[4]

His superior's demands on Padre Pio persisted. His superior cared for him, but expected much from the young priest. Padre Benedetto, however, gave Padre Pio permission to conclude his religious education under archpriest Don Pannullo in Pietrelcina. Padre Pio was grateful.

During Padre Pio's stay in Pietrelcina, he often exchanged letter writings with other superiors. Padre Agostino was one of them. The devil continued to interfere with the written communication between Padre Pio and his superiors. In 1912, Padre Agostino wanted to test the young priest's holiness and beset the devil. He began to write to Padre Pio in French and Greek. Padre Pio didn't understand either language. Padre Pio explained to Padre Pannullo what the letter was about. He passed the foreign languages tests with flying colors. In 1919, Padre Pannullo wrote a letter under oath stating that this was true.

He further verified this extraordinary experience when Padre Agostino had asked him how he learned the two languages. Padre Pio responded with the words of Jeremiah, "Ah, Lord God, I do not know how to speak."[5]

Padre Agostino in his <u>Diario</u> (diary) said.

"Padre Pio does not understand either Greek or French. His guardian angel explained everything to him and he replied to me in like manners."[6]

The holiness of Padre Pio was evident and the help that his celestial friend gave was most endearing.

While in Pietrelcina, Padre Pio said mass every day at church. Some residents of Pietrelcina were less than pleased. The people complained that he prayed too much and that his masses were too long. They grumbled that the three-hour mass kept them from fieldwork.

When Padre Pio was in deep prayers at Pianna Romana, children would sneak up and spy on him. The young people made fun of his religious ways. They often called him a wild monk.

Other people thought he had tuberculosis and kept their distances from him. Parents wouldn't allow Padre Pio to come to their houses because of his health problems. They were terrified that he'd infect their children. Father Pannullo's relatives were uncomfortable with Padre Pio. Whenever he came to the house, Father Pannullo's nieces would ask Padre Pio to use the same chair. Once, the bishop of Benevento, Italy came to see Father Pannullo and invited Padre Pio to dinner and reflections. When Father Pannullo's niece heard about the invited guest, she made a big fuss. Padre Pio stayed away.

The Pannullo family continued to make problems. The last straw for Padre Pio was an incident during his mass. Another niece insisted that Padre Pio use his own garments and chalice. When she noticed that he wasn't using the chalice chosen for him, the mass was stopped and the right chalice was brought in. Padre Pio had had enough! He didn't mince his words in speaking to Father Pannullo. He explained to the old priest that the Lord had assured him that his health problems were not contagious. His situation improved.

Padre Pio felt distressed with the humiliations. He continued to show kindness when others didn't. He was there to do God's work and nothing would stop him.

World War I was to intervene in his life and the lives of many people.

On November 6, 1915, Padre Pio went to Benevento, Italy for military services. He was drafted in the Italian army and World War I. The army stationed him to the 10th Company of the Medical Corps in Naples, Italy. He worked on the clean-up unit and running errands. The uniform the Italian army gave him was much too big. He couldn't stand wearing it. It had nothing to do with his loyalty to the Italian army. He just wished he didn't have to wear it. Due to his religious belief, he was uncomfortable without his Capuchin habit. Again, he experienced loneliness and depression.

He wasn't a well man, but the Italian army had little regard for his health or depression. Shortly after, Padre Pio became sick. Once again, he couldn't hold down any food. He was drained of his physical energy. His army superiors became concerned, and a requisition for further examinations was written up. The doctors found that Padre Pio had a serious form of bronchitis.

The Italian army asked Padre Pio to stay at a hotel in Naples, Italy. Since he didn't have any money, his parents had to foot the bill for the food and hotel stay. Finally, the Italian army sent Padre Pio to Pietrelcina for health reasons. The army gave him six months leave of absence. He was relieved and thanked God for His mercy.

Meanwhile, the Capuchin Order wanted Padre Pio back at the monastery. Many priests from the order were called to war. The monastery was almost empty. In the past, Padre Benedetto had only suggested that Padre Pio return to community life. With the war situation, he became more demanding. Padre Pio resisted due to his health problems.

Meanwhile, Padre Agostino, another of Padre Pio's superiors wrote to him on December 20, 1915. He accused the young priest of to much attachment to his hometown. Padre Benedetto also wrote to him on December 24, 1915. The letter stated that it wasn't proper for a priest to stay home for medical reasons.

Padre Pio accused Padre Agostino of not understanding the depth of his medical problems and just wanting him back at the monastery. He went on to say that Padre Benedetto hadn't ordered him under obedience; therefore, he didn't have to return!

Obedience is one of the vows most religious orders have. By taking the vow of obedience, the religious promises God to follow the rules of their orders. The superior is the person who's given the authority to guide the religious to follow the rules.

The demands kept pouring in.

Padre Agostino traveled to Pietrelcina to see Padre Pio. He met an unfriendly town. Despite their earlier treatment of him, the people of Pietrelcina had grown to love and respect Padre Pio's holiness. They didn't want Padre Pio to go back. A riot almost ensued within the city! Father Pannullo had to be called to talk some sense into the townspeople. At one point, Padre Agostine was even threatened if he dared take Padre Pio from Pietrelcina.

Mrs. Forgione spoke to Padre Agostino regarding her son's possible departure to the community life. Padre Agostino told Mrs. Forgione that Padre Pio belonged to the Capuchin Order. Padre Agostino also added that she had to let go of Padre Pio. As hard as it was for Mrs. Forgione, she loosened her grip on her son.

But Padre Pio continued to have misgivings on returning to the religious community life. Padre Pio was afraid his health problems would return once he stepped into the monastery.

Padre Agostino left Pietrelcina. Shortly after, he wrote to Padre Pio and persuaded him to visit a sick woman in Foggia, Italy. On February 1916, Padre Pio agreed to make the visit. Once he arrived, he met Padre Benedetto at the friary. Padre Benedetto ordered Padre Pio to remain at the friary. Padre Benedetto demanded that the young priest write to his mom for his belongings!

Padre Pio stayed at a friary in Foggia, Italy for some time. He was sick and again couldn't hold down any food. His concerns about his health were right. Padre Pio's health became worse as soon as he entered the monastery.

During the summer of 1916, Padre Pio visited the monastery of San Giovanni Rotondo to see a friend. He loved the location and the fresh air. It suited him.

In 1916, San Giovanni Rotondo had about twelve thousand people. It was between sixteen and two thousand feet above sea level in the Gargano Mountains. In those days, the people didn't have modern conveniences. Clothes had to be washed by hands. Their water supply was from a stream or well. The people worked hard without anything to show for their work. Poverty followed their every step. Traveling was either by walking, riding the mules, or if one was lucky, a buggy.

The friary of Our Lady of Grace in San Giovanni Rotondo was very poor. It was built in 1540. In 1624, strong earthquake destroyed it. It was rebuilt. In 1676, a new church also was constructed. It adjoined the new friary.

On September 1916, Padre Pio moved there. The Capuchin community had seven priests. Padre Pio was made to feel welcome at his new home. He not only taught the young seminarians but also provided spiritual guidance to them.

The young seminarians loved him. He was a good teacher and the seminarians related well to him. He also spoke to them very kindly.

He had a gift with the young and the old. He reached out with sincerity, love and respect. Most people responded in kind.

Miscommunication once again came to the forefront.

On August 19, 1917, he returned to Naples, Italy for military services. He received a surprise once he arrived. The Italian army had made plans to arrest him for desertion. The original telegram send to San Giovanni Rotondo was in Padre Pio's family name of Francesco Forgione. Since the religious at San Giovanni Rotondo didn't recognize the name, the telegram was returned. Padre Pio explained to his army superiors that he was known as Padre Pio of Pietrelcina, not Francesco Forgione. Shortly after, he was again giving a leave of absence for health problems.

On March 5, 1918 he attempted to continue his military duties in Naples, Italy. He came down with double pneumonia. When the Italian army learned of this, he was given a final discharge on March 16, 1918. He was 31 years old.

Padre Pio wasn't happy in the army, but he gave it his best. Although he felt humiliated by the army's ways and constant medical examinations, he wanted to go back to his ministry. Padre Pio was prepared for whatever was to be.

Before going back to San Giovanni Rotondo, he visited with his family in Pietrelcina. It was the last time he went back to his hometown. Padre Pio returned to his beloved monastery to complete his Master's work.

The rose was blooming.

CHAPTER 4

News of Padre Pio's holiness was spreading all over Italy and the world. He preferred the privacy of the monastery in San Giovanni Rotondo, where he could work night and day to bring people from all stations of life closer to the Lord. His health continued to go up and down. He felt physical pains just like any other human being. He dealt with his lot in life the best he could.

Padre Pio also connected with his spiritual children. They consisted of the young and old. The spiritual children learned to follow Padre Pio's holy ways. He guided them through their spiritual needs. At first he was gentle in teaching about Jesus. He even passed out candy. Once he knew that his spiritual children were bonding with God, he became demanding in his teaching and their responsibilities toward the Catholic faith. As a result, people found their ways to the Lord.

He even exchanged letters with the spiritual children who lived outside of San Giovanni Rotondo. Padre Pio was meticulous or careful with his correspondence. He wanted to reach out to everyone about the greatness of the Lord. He wanted to bring people to God. This was the goal that stayed in Padre Pio's mind, soul and body twenty-four hours a day.

One day a Visitor came with His rays of light.

On August 5, 1918, while Padre Pio was hearing confession, he suddenly felt afraid. He stopped the confession and sent the young seminarian away. Padre Pio saw a heavenly figure outside the confessional with a sharp spear. This figure was Jesus and He pierced Padre Pio's heart. This is called the transverberation of the heart.

On August 5, 1918 Padre Pio wrote to Padre Benedetto regarding the transverberation of the heart:

> ...Everything inside of me is raining blood, and sometimes even my bodily eyes are forced to submit to look on the bloody torrent of this stream...Stop this torture for me, this condemnation, this humiliation, this confusion. My soul can no longer endure it...[1]

Padre Pio's suffering from the transverberation of the heart continued for days. His pains were not only unbearable, but Padre Pio had a difficult time dealing with the physical and emotional suffering.

Again, the Visitor arrived.

On September 20, 1918 while praying after mass in a section of the church called the choir, Padre Pio became drowsy. Silence and peace surrounded him. A mysterious man came before Padre Pio. It was the same person who had visited the priest on August 5, 1918. The appearance of the mysterious man was different. He dripped blood from his hands, feet and side. Padre Pio was scared by all that he saw. The vision disappeared and Padre Pio noticed that his own hands, feet and side were dripping blood. Padre Pio had received the stigmata or the five wounds of Jesus. Only Jesus gives the stigmata, but the Blessed Mother honored the young priest with her presence.

After the Lord had left, Padre Pio could not get up. He was filled with pain, shock and weakness. Somehow, he made it to his cell and attempted to clean the wounds. When he saw the bloody wounds, he cried. He felt unworthy of such an honor. Padre Pio praised Jesus for the gifts He had bestowed on him. He prayed for nine days and told no one about the wounds. Padre Pio asked the Lord to take them away. God told him the wounds would stay.

On October 22, 1918, Padre Pio had this to say in a letter to his Spiritual Director: "...I noticed that my hands and feet and chest had been pierced and were bleeding profusely. Imagine the confusion which I experienced then and which I experience continuously almost every day."[2]

The stigmatist thought he was going to die from the excessive bleeding.

Only Padre Benedetto, Padre Paolino and few others knew that Padre Pio had received the stigmata. He would cover the wounds with his sleeves, but his limping was difficult to hide. He would apply iodine on his wounds in hope that they would heal and go away. They bled constantly.

Life at the monastery went on as usual. Everyone had their work to do. Even though Padre Pio's physical disabilities were extraordinary; he continued his duties. His faith carried him through the darkest of nights. He continued to clean the wounds himself as best he could. Yet knowledge of the stigmatic young priest crept outside the monastery of San Giovanni Rotondo and elsewhere.

Padre Pio's religious views continued. He didn't want to bring attention to himself. However, the rule of obedience came into focus. Padre Pio was "Son of obedience."[3]

A fellow priest told Padre Pio that his superior wanted his pictures taken. Padre Pio didn't object. He was jovial and comfortable with this. The stigmatized priest obeyed orders with his famous humor and gentleness.

Padre Placido took the first photos of Padre Pio in the monastery's courtyard. The first picture showed the wounds on his hands. The second photo showed the young priest holding a lamb.

Pandemonium did follow the appearance of the stigmata. All the commotion was difficult for Padre Pio to fathom. He wanted privacy. He wasn't giving the freedom or time to adjust to his situation.

The Capuchin Order had a new round of doctors examine Padre Pio's wounds. The doctors described how deep the lesions were.

Padre Pio obeyed the new orders for the medical exams, but wasn't happy about them.

On July 26, 1919, the Vatican also sent their physician to examine the wounds and formulate the results. Dr. Bignami was a well-known pathologist in Rome, Italy. He examined Padre Pio and concluded that the application of iodine could have caused the irritations of the wounds. Dr. Bignami applied salve or ointment on the lesions and wrapped them in bandages. The doctor added nothing else to his report. The Capuchin Order was not happy with this conclusion.

Padre Pio wasn't jumping for joy, either.

The general superiors of the Capuchin Order in Rome requested that another physician check Padre Pio. On October 9, 1919, Dr. Festa, a surgeon, was asked to examine him. The examinations were long and difficult. The doctor tried to be fair in the medical findings. The lesions, he concluded were a true form of the stigmata.

Shortly after, the Vatican wouldn't allow anyone to examine the wounds of Padre Pio without their permission. The stigmatized priest was relieved.

He kept his humor despite his circumstances. When the occasion arose, he said it like it was.

Once, a gentleman came to see Padre Pio. He told Padre Pio that a physician had a message for him. The gentleman said that Padre Pio had the wounds of Jesus due to his constant attention to the Crucifix and Passion.

The stigmatized priest responded, "Tell them go out to the fields. Look at, concentrate on the bull there, then see if they grow horns!"[4]

Later, Dr. Festa operated twice on Padre Pio, but not on the lesions. On October 25, 1925, Dr. Festa took out Padre Pio's hernia. It was a necessary surgery. Dr. Festa didn't have the time to request permission from The Holy See. In deference or respect to the Church, Padre Pio refused anesthesia. He also wanted to offer the suffering to the Lord. Padre Pio accepted a sip of liqueur. The priest joked that if he were put under anesthesia, Dr. Festa would continue to examine his wounds. He fainted during the surgery. Dr. Festa observed his lesions. In 1927, the doctor removed a cyst on Padre Pio's neck. Again, he refused anesthesia.

He didn't like to take time off even for medical reasons. In fact, after his second surgery, he went right back to his religious duties.

Padre Pio's persistence and faith carried him through those demanding times. He respected the authority of his superiors. Time spent toward his religious responsibilities were of utmost importance, but Padre Pio wouldn't think of disobeying orders. That didn't mean he wasn't assertive. He expressed his opinions on many issues throughout his life as a Capuchin priest. This was especially true when people didn't follow the ways of Jesus. He wanted people to be sincere and true toward the path to God.

Because of the pressures and desire to be with God, the stigmatic priest often prayed to be called to his heavenly home. His physical pains were so great that he became discouraged. Even though he called upon heaven to call him, it was not to be. God had plans for Padre Pio. His time had not come.

The Heavenly Father continued to give Padre Pio His love, strength and drive to keep going. The Lord stayed by Padre Pio's side and gently but firmly showed His ways.

From 1919 to 1931 difficult circumstances were to make his life even more unbearable for Padre Pio. He lived by his strong faith. He kept silence although chaos surrounded him. Padre Pio prayed and worked toward the goals that Jesus had for him.

In April of 1920, Padre Pio had a surprise visitor. Dr. Gemelli was a priest and well- known doctor and psychologist who didn't care for Padre Pio. Dr. Gemelli went to the monastery of San Giovanni Rotondo in an attempt to examine Padre Pio. He was refused. Dr. Gemelli didn't have written permission from the Vatican or the Capuchin Order. Padre Pio felt that without written permission, he didn't have to be examined by the doctor. His superiors at San Giovanni Rotondo supported him. Padre Pio didn't mince his words when refusing Dr. Gemelli. Afterwards, Padre Pio walked out of the meeting. Padre Pio was becoming tired of being examined over and over. He wanted peace and quiet to continue his work.

Dr. Gemelli later wrote that St. Francis of Assisi was the only true stigmatic. Any other stigmatics weren't on the up and up. Despite Dr. Gemelli's rash writing, Pope Benedict XV gave Padre Pio his continuous support.

Most popes believed that Padre Pio was a servant of the Lord. Pope Benedict XV respected and protected Padre Pio. However, after Pope Benedict passed away, Pope Pius XI became the leader of the Catholic Church. He was also a close friend of Dr. Gemelli. Pope Pius XI had great admiration for Padre Pio, but truthful people didn't always surround him. Those individuals didn't always present the Pope with the facts about Padre Pio.

Other individuals who worked against Padre Pio were Archbishop Gagliardi of Manfredonia, Italy, Father Miscio and Father Palladino. They didn't speak kindly of Padre Pio. They wrote letters to the Vatican against him. Some even presented themselves to representatives of Pope Pius XI. These individuals were afraid of the goodness that Padre Pio stood for. Padre Pio maintained silence against his attackers.

Finally, the Vatican got involved and investigated. Unfortunately, Padre Pio's adversaries were invited, too. The results of that investigation were to put restrictions on Padre Pio's religious life.

CHAPTER 5

In 1920, rumors that Padre Pio was going to be transferred led to a riot in San Giovanni Rotondo. Before the riot ended, six people had died and many were injured.

The Holy See became upset with all the problems at San Giovanni Rotondo.

After the 1922 Vatican's investigation, Padre Pio was restricted. He had to say mass in a private chapel at various hours. The times of the masses were not announced. Permission to hear confession was also denied. This was a loss for the people who needed his guidance. He wasn't even allowed to bless the crowd from his window. The stigmatist was not permitted to write to his spiritual children and this restriction remained for the rest of his life. Padre Pio was also to be transferred to the northern part of Italy.

The Vatican felt that if the source of trouble were removed, peace would be restored. They recommended that clergy and people not visit San Giovanni Rotondo. The Vatican felt that Padre Pio was useless and a fraud.

People in San Giovanni Rotondo rebelled. No one was going to take Padre Pio from them. People from all over the area came to the monastery to protest the possible move.

The residents of San Giovanni Rotondo carried torches and weapons. Guards were posted at the monastery on a twenty-four hour basis. Some protesters tried to burn down houses of clergy who had given Padre Pio a difficult time. Mayor Morcaldi was able to talk them out of any destructive moves.

Poor Padre Pio almost became a victim of the flowing storms. He was threatened during one of his services. An emotional laborer from the vicinity ran up to the priest and held a gun to his head. The laborer told Padre Pio that he was going to stay at the friary either dead or alive. Luckily, the man was restrained, but the stigmatized priest was visibly shaken by the episode.

On August 23, 1923, Padre Pio wrote to Mayor Morcaldi of San Giovanni Rotondo. He expressed his concerns about everyone's safety. The good priest also felt bad that the demonstrations were caused by his possible departure from the friary.

The letter to the mayor continued expressing his appreciation for the people of San Giovanni Rotondo. He also made a request, which showed his love for his people. The letter concluded:

> I will always remember these generous people in my poor and assiduous prayers imploring peace and prosperity for them...being unable to do anything else, I express the desire, that if my superiors are not opposed, my bones be placed in a tranquil corner of this land.[1]

The Vatican received word of what was going on in San Giovanni Rotondo. A meeting was held with the top people in the Vatican. The transfer of Padre Pio was stopped on August 17, 1923.

Once Padre Pio found out that he was not to be transferred, he went to the window and announced to his people the good news. Cheering and applause followed.

Although the people of San Giovanni Rotondo were happy, they were still skeptical. Individuals still kept a vigil by the monastery. After a week or so, they relaxed a bit, but the enforcement around the friary remained.

The fight was not over. The Vatican gave in a bit, but the restrictions lingered. The peace that Padre Pio so desired was not to be.

Was Padre Pio upset about the restrictions? Yes, indeed. He was crushed when the Vatican transferred Padre Benedetto, who had been his good friend and spiritual director for many years. The Vatican did not allow them to speak again.

Padre Pio accepted all these sorrows and continued the Lord's work the best way he could. He chose Padre Agostino as his new Spiritual Director.

Pope Pius XI was busy with other matters of the Catholic Church. He formed a committee to look into the life and ways of Padre Pio. Unfortunately, Dr. Gemelli and Monsignor Gagliardi were part of this group.

Dr. Gemelli related to the Holy See that he had examined Padre Pio's wounds. The examination never took place.

Monsignor Gagliardi reported to the Vatican that Padre Pio's tone and attitude upset the people during the Sacrament of Confession. He also accused Padre Pio and his fellow friars of taking money given to the church. False reports that Padre Pio was not following orders also reached Rome.

Padre Pio fell into a deep depression. He accepted God's will during these difficult times, but he felt very alone. He continued to offer his work and heartaches to the Lord.

On June of 1931 the Vatican acted again.

Padre Pio was stripped of all his priestly duties with the exception of saying mass. He was to stay in his room and not have any contacts with people. Only the altar servers were to help with his mass in the morning. The younger seminarian students didn't want to assist at his mass. The masses were long and Padre Pio often went into ecstasy with Jesus, the Blessed Mother and Heavenly Hosts. The students had studies and other tasks to complete. Padre Pio bribed them with candy. A two-hour limit was given for mass. Padre Pio's library time was only for an hour or so.

The chapel that the stigmatist used for mass had an altar, crucifix, a picture of the Blessed Mother and two chairs. Padre Pio felt joy and happiness in the beauty and isolation of the chapel. Yet, continued to feel deep sorrows for what the Catholic Church was doing to him.

This went on for two long years! The grieving priest was a prisoner in his own monastery.

On July 1, 1931, Padre Agostino went to San Giovanni Rotondo to speak with Padre Pio. Padre Pio was upset and depressed with the restraints from the Vatican. Padre Pio began crying as soon as they entered his room.

Padre Agostino described Padre Pio's emotional state in his <u>Diario</u> (diary):

> ...Although deeply affected by this, I was able to quell my own emotions and let him cry for some time. Afterwards we talked. Dear Padre Pio told me that he was quite affected by this unexpected trial...Padre Pio answered, "I never thought that this would happen..."[2]

July 24, 1931, Padre Agostino went back to see his friend. In light of the difficulties, Padre Pio continued to have a wonderful sense of humor.

Padre Agostino again writes in his Diario of this account:

> ...On July 24, 1931, I returned to San Giovanni Rotondo...How do you spend your days? I questioned him. I study as much as I can, and then I annoy my brothers, he answered. How is this possible? I asked. As

always, I tell them jokes, and the jokes are even worse than before...[3]

In the early 1930's rumors that Padre Pio was to be transferred upset his followers. Everyone was concerned that the riot and bloodshed of 1920 would happen again.

Pius XI felt bad for Padre Pio. He told the archbishop of Manfredonia, Italy, "I have not been badly disposed toward Padre Pio, but I have been badly informed about Padre Pio."[4] In 1933, the Pope lifted the restrictions.

Padre Pio was allowed to once again say mass in the church. He was also allowed to hear confession a year later. People were overjoyed that the restrictions had been removed. His enemies continued to roar, but they couldn't destroy the work the Lord set forth for Padre Pio.

CHAPTER 6

In the early 1930's, Padre Pio continued to be misunderstood and misjudged. He was a great believer that heartaches brought us closer to the Lord. The priest assured his followers that sufferings were not a punishment from Jesus, but a blessing.

He believed that the way people carried the trials and tribulations of life showed how much we loved God. On the other hand, if people complained, cried or beat their chests, they lost the grace and ability to get closer to the Lord.

On November 1931, Padre Pio shared a deep-felt fear with his friend, Padre Agostino, "I would rather die a thousand times than make up my mind to offend God who is so good."[1]

It frustrated him, not knowing where he stood on his state of grace with God. The Lord kept his silence. He told his friend that if the Lord would honor his request to know where he stood, his work would be even better. After taking about it, Padre Agostino felt that Padre Pio was ready to accept the Lord's will.

Although Padre Pio's enemies gave him grief, his many friends loved and protected him. He had many friends who cared about his happiness. A few went overboard.

Padre Pio loved and prayed for his boyhood friends from Pietrelcina. Once he entered the religious life, Padre Benedetto and Padre Agostino made a great impact on his life.

44

Although he was able to confide more to Padre Benedetto of his feelings for God and the Blessed Mother, it was Padre Agostino who continued to write down accounts of Padre Pio's ecstasy with our Lord and the Blessed Mother.

When Padre Pio was enraptured with his Heavenly Visits, he didn't hear anything else. However, if his spiritual directors mentally asked Padre Pio that he had to come back to the present under obedience, the stigmatist would do so. This showed how much he respected the orders of his earthly superiors.

Padre Paolino was a lifelong friend of Padre Pio. Under Holy Obedience, Padre Pio told his friend about the stigmata. Padre Paolino was so excited about the news that he told his sister. Afterwards, the news leaked out to the media. Since the Holy See and the Capuchin Order wanted this to be kept quiet, Padre Paolino was approached about his behavior. This didn't help Padre Pio's cause.

Miss Mary McAlpin Pyle was a good friend of Padre Pio. Their friendship began in 1925 and continued until her death on April 26, 1968. She was a wealthy American who became a spiritual child of the priest. Miss Pyle donated her own money for Padre Pio's many causes.

Miss Pyle had been baptized in the Presbyterian Church in New York. Prior to meeting Padre Pio, she was influenced by Maria Montessori to reach out to the Catholic Church. When Miss Pyle met Padre Pio, he asked her to stay in San Giovanni Rotondo. Miss Pyle tried to go back to Rome with her friend, Ms. Montessori, but couldn't. Padre Pio's humility and love had touched her.

She built a pink house in town and joined the ministry of Padre Pio. With the much-loved stigmatist's blessing and the permission of the Capuchin Order, Miss Pyle joined The Third Order of St. Francis. The order was available to lay people who were not in the formal religious order. She further received permission to wear the habit of this prestigious religious order.

For quite a while, the people of San Giovanni Rotondo resented and shunned Miss Pyle. The people refused to sit with her at church services. Some called her unkind names. They blamed her in part for the Holy See's investigation of Padre Pio. They accused Miss Pyle of using the media to spread his miracles and cures. The residents felt she had spoken in excess.

This brought added sadness to Padre Pio.

Miss Pyle prayed that the investigation against her friend would come to an end. She praised God when the Vatican removed some of the restrictions. Shortly after, a group from Pietrelcina approached Miss Pyle on building a monastery there. She went to the mystic and he quickly answered, "Do it at once and let it be dedicated to the Holy Family."[2]

After receiving feedback from Padre Pio, she agreed to give her financial support. Miss Pyle also paid for a seminary. The ground breaking for both buildings took place in 1926. Padre Pio's prophecy of years past had come true!

Because of problems with the diocese, the monastery wasn't used by the Capuchin religious until later.

Although Miss Pyle went through her own hardship, she continued working for forty years in Padre Pio's ministry. The town's people eventually came around and welcomed Miss Pyle as one of their own.

Emmanuele Brunnatto was another friend. He loved the good life until Padre Pio touched his heart. After he met Padre Pio, he changed his life style. Mr. Brunnatto devoted his time to Padre Pio's ministry. He met Francesco Morcaldi, the mayor of San Giovanni Rotondo. Together, they tried to help Padre Pio when the Vatican put restrictions on him.

Mr. Brunnatto and Mr. Morcaldi, the town's mayor, were present when the Vatican had investigated Padre Pio. However, these two friends were over diligent in their efforts to free Padre Pio from the Vatican's harshness. Whenever the opportunities came up, both men spoke against the injustices the Holy See's was aiming at Padre Pio. Padre Pio was not only caught in the middle, but the efforts of his friends placed him in a negative light with Rome.

A few people at the Vatican felt genuinely bad for everything that was happening to Padre Pio, but the enemies were greater in power.

Shortly after, in 1932, the Vatican issued another restriction.

The Holy See moved The Seraphic College out of San Giovanni Rotondo. Padre Pio was devastated. He had acted as a spiritual director at the college for years and missed teaching the young people.

Mr. Brunnatto believed that the restrictions against Padre Pio were wrong. Therefore, Brunnatto threatened to publish unfavorable information regarding higher ups in the Catholic Church if they weren't removed. This didn't go well with the Vatican. Pope Pius XI send two trusted individuals to San Giovanni Rotondo to spend time with and observe Padre Pio. Their names were Monsignors Luca Pasetto and Felice Bevilacqua.

Both Monsignors met and spoke to Padre Pio about the Vatican's concerns. They liked what they saw. The gentlemen found Padre Pio to be a loving, kind and caring priest. Padre Pio shared his concern about Mr. Brunnatto and offered to write to him.

The stigmatist's communication with Mr. Brunnatto fell on deaf ears. He held steadfast to his threats.

Meanwhile, Monsignors Pasetto and Bevilacqua reported back to Pope Pius XI on Padre Pio. They assured the Pope that he was a man of great holiness and cared greatly for the well being of the Catholic Church. Pope Pius XI appreciated the clarity and honesty of their convictions.

Mr. Brunnatto didn't carry through with his threats. Any information he had on Vatican's officials wasn't published. Nonetheless, the Capuchin Order resented his behavior. They made it known that he wouldn't be welcomed in their monastery.

The women of San Giovanni Rotondo loved Padre Pio, but at times added their own selfish input into the troubled times. They became demanding and jealous if their time with the holy priest was curtailed. The women wanted to be close to Padre Pio in confession and at mass. They pushed and shoved others aside for a seat closer to the altar. The women also got into fights when confession time came around.

People saw Padre Pio as a holy man, but many also viewed him as a celebrity. People wanted to overtake his life. The peace and quiet Padre Pio needed for his ministry certainly wasn't coming his way.

Many times Padre Pio was fenced in as he made attempts to walk to various areas of the church. The holy women would cut areas of his religious habit and Franciscan cord. He would often tell them to move away. Men sold parts of his clothes for relics by dousing them in chickens' blood. A relic is a keepsake or cherished belongings of an individual. People sold prayer cards with Padre Pio's picture on them. Others tried to grab his stigmatized hands to kiss. Since his hands were always swollen from the wounds, this act was extremely painful for him. The friars working as his guards often had difficulty protecting him from the enthusiastic crowds.

The Capuchin Order didn't want the Vatican to make further problems for Padre Pio. An internal investigation was made. They questioned some of his female followers. Padre Pio's routine was made less stressful for a while.

Another friend was to be instrumental in helping Padre Pio accomplish a long held goal. Padre Pio was always concerned about the lack of medical facilities in San Giovanni Rotondo. Many people had to go to nearby cities for serious medical help. Often, they didn't make it because of the distance or severity of their conditions. He wanted to build a hospital to ease the problems.

He believed that Jesus was in the hearts and soul of individuals that were ill. He saw Christ's image in everyone. He felt that when individuals were poor and sick, the Lord suffered even more. As a result, Padre Pio wanted them to be treated as a whole.

Padre Pio didn't want to call it a hospital, but instead a home. The stigmatist wanted physicians to heal the medical problems and priests to give them spiritual help. It was very important to him that individuals worked with acts of love and charity toward the sick. Patients, he felt, would heal sooner.

In the early 1930's, Padre Pio wanted Dr. Sanguinetti to help him build the hospital called, Home for the Relief of Suffering. Due to economic reasons, his good friend wasn't comfortable leaving his medical practice. Padre Pio assured him that God would take care of him. Shortly after, the doctor received a financial blessing. The loyal doctor came and helped build the hospital. Dr. Sanguinetti was the first Medical Director.

The doctor was one of Padre Pio's closest friends. Padre Pio was hurt that the Lord didn't forewarn him of Dr. Sanguinetti's death.

God gave the stigmatist warnings on so many other matters, but the impending death of his dear friend was kept from him.

The hospital was completed two years later. It was dedicated on May 5, 1956. It remains the finest hospital in Italy.

Padre Pio made many friends in the Capuchin Order throughout his life. Many Capuchins assisted Padre Pio. His spiritual children throughout the world loved this dear man.

Despite all the caring people that surrounded the mystic, some of the restrictions remained. The following restrictions were enforced for the rest of his life. He couldn't talk to women going or coming from the confessional or church. His meetings with men in the monastery's hall were limited.

The media weren't friendly to Padre Pio. Their behavior and actions made it difficult for him. The media weren't welcome at the monastery. When they closed in on Padre Pio, he would often yell, "Let me through!"[3]

The world chose to bestow a celebrity status on Padre Pio. He didn't want any part of that! Often he would become very frustrated with the over zealous crowd.

The insanity that surrounded Padre Pio intensified as it closed in around him.

Mrs. Vera Calandra (left) of the National Centre for Padre Pio with Elvira Mucciarone Janz (author) observing the picture of St. Pio

St. Pio celebrating Mass
Courtesy of Edizioni "Padre Pio di Pietrelcina"

St. Pio in a lighter moment
Courtesy of Edizioni "Padre Pio di Pietrelcina"

St. Pio in a reflective mood wearing the Capuchin Habit
Courtesy of Edizioni "Padre Pio di Pietrelcina"

Miracle survivor, Paul Walsh (upper right) pictured with nephews and nieces

Paul and Mrs. Walsh (mother) celebrating his birthday

Jacob Hefer (right) miracle survivor, with his brother and baby sister

CHAPTER 7

While the bickering amongst his enemies and friends continued, Padre Pio went on with his work to the best of his abilities. His work and prayers were nonstop.

In 1933, despite Padre Pio's forced reclusion, pilgrimages continued coming. The busses had fewer pilgrimages, but they still drove up to the monastery in San Giovanni Rotondo. They didn't care that the Vatican had discouraged visiting the holy priest. His people wanted to see him.

He was very much aware of the distractions. It was a real concern for him.

When Padre Pio would see the crowds from his window, he would pray, "Jesus, these people, what do they want of me."[1]

He didn't realize the people were there to see him. The crowds puzzled him. People throughout the world knew that Padre Pio stood for goodness and kindness, and that he was a true representative of God's love. The stigmatist never fully realized the impact he made in people's lives. People who loved him needed to be near such a pure, loving and powerful individual.

Still, Padre Pio had his fears.

He worried that the crowds would get out of control. Padre Pio didn't want any added problems. His memories of past riots were still vivid.

The apprehensive priest was also concerned that the influx of people would take him away from his religious responsibilities. Although Padre Pio had all these internal and external concerns, he reached out to people in need.

The honorable and softhearted priest touched gently but powerfully upon the lives of children, too.

Padre Pio loved children with all his heart. People used to present him with gifts of chocolates and various candies. He did not indulge, but saved them for others. He enjoyed giving them to the little ones. Padre Pio would also give them sugar cubes. The compassionate stigmatist would "bless the sugar cubes and pass them out to the children."[2]

In the 1930's and on, his family would often come to see Padre Pio. On one particular occasion, Padre Pio had a dinner set out in the dining room for them. Everyone had a good time eating and catching up on news. Padre Pio noticed that the young six-year old nephew was bored. He got up and went to another area of the room and signaled Ettoruccio to come over. Padre Pio carried him to his room and gave him sweets. Later, the little boy told the family how kind Padre Pio was.

In 1933, Padre Pio was sick in bed for a whole week. It was the Holy Week before Easter. His temperature was 116 degrees Fahrenheit. A kitchen thermometer was used to check his fever. A normal thermometer would just break!

He was upset with the imposed restrictions, but when others were in pain he was moved to help.

Padre Pio was a miracle worker of children. Whenever he interceded to God for a particular miracle, he offered himself as sacrifice. Padre Pio had high fevers, stomach trouble and terrible headaches. These and other physical ailments occurred each time that he asked the Lord for miracles. The Lord accepted his requests but his sufferings were difficult. He, however, did not give up. Padre Pio kept his suffering and prayers going until God granted the miracles.

In 1920 when Padre Pio was thirty-three years old, an unusual miracle involving a child occurred through his intercession. Years later, Ms. Agata Panunzio, wrote a letter thanking God and Padre Pio.

Agata Panunzio came down with a rash on her head. Her mother took her to many specialists. They couldn't find a cure for the rash. To prevent further infections, her hair was shaved. Agata was upset about the baldness.

Finally, Agata's mother took her daughter to San Giovanni Rotondo where relatives lived. Agata's aunt was washing the woolen gloves of Padre Pio. When her aunt had finished, she washed Agata's head with the same water used to wash Padre Pio's gloves. Throughout, the aunt kept praying to Padre Pio for his intercession.

A moment later, the aunt looked at her niece's head. Agata's rash was gone.

On February 1933, a small boy named Sergio was sick with influenza. This is a highly contagious infection attacking the lungs. It is caused by a virus and transmitted by air-borne particles. Sergio had stayed in bed for sometime. The young boy began vomiting. During the night, Sergio's father dreamed of Padre Pio. The mystic told him, "I have cured your child of a very grave malady."[3] The father went to check on his son. Sergio was resting comfortably. The next morning, the little boy wanted to go to school.

Many times, the individuals involved in the miracle thanked Padre Pio. He told the people to thank God who allowed the miracle to take place. Padre Pio always emphasized that the honor and glory should go to our Lord Jesus. Not once did he take the credit for any miracles.

Padre Pio didn't discuss the miracles. When people questioned him about them, he was embarrassed. If people insisted, Padre Pio would give a pointed and short response.

The following miracle is another example of Padre Pio's powerful intercession. Gemma Di Giorgi was born on Dec. 25, 1940 in Ribera, Sicily. She was born without pupils in her eyes. The eye specialists couldn't do anything. Gemma's family accepted the news, but her grandmother refused. On June 6, 1946, Gemma and her grandmother made a long pilgrimage to San Giovanni Rotondo to see Padre Pio. Gemma was six years old.

They attended Padre Pio's mass. At the end of the mass Padre Pio called out for the little girl by her name. Gemma's grandmother walked up to the front of the altar with her granddaughter. There, they came face to face with the stigmatized priest.

Padre Pio was gentle with Gemma. The affectionate priest wanted Gemma to make her First Communion. He heard her confession in the Sacrament of Penance. Afterwards, Padre Pio placed his hands on the little girl's eyes. Gemma went on to receive the First Holy Communion.

Later, Gemma's grandmother asked her if she had asked Padre Pio for any graces. It had slipped the little girl's mind.

Shortly after, Padre Pio came upon them and said: "May the Madonna bless you, Gemma. Be a good girl!"[4]

Seconds later, Gemma began to cry. She was able to see!

Gemma had received a miracle from God through the intercession of Padre Pio. Doctors examined her and couldn't find any medical explanations. The little girl without the pupils in her eyes could see for the first time in her young life. This blessing of sight continued throughout her life.

The following grace was bestowed on the little boy through the prayers and intercession of Padre Pio. Gianfranco Cuccoli of Italy was four years old. For over two weeks, he had suffered from peritonitis. This is an inflammation of the peritoneum. The peritoneum is the membrane lining the walls of the abdominal cavity, which encloses the intestines.

Mrs. Cuccoli wrote to the friary asking Padre Pio's prayers and intercession for her little boy. A response was received. It stated that Padre Pio would pray for his recovery.

Later, the little boy's fever was a concern for the family. The physician came to examine Gianfranco, again. The doctor told the mother that her son had bronchial pneumonia as a result of meningitis. He prescribed a different medication. He told Gianfranco's mother that if his young patient wasn't better by the next day, he would be placed in the hospital.

Gianfranco's mother wrote to Padre Pio again. She continued to pray to the kind stigmatist for her young son. Mrs. Cuccoli also placed a picture of Padre Pio under the little boy's pillow.

Gianfranco prayed to Padre Pio to make him better. The little one had his own faith in the knowledgeable priest.

The mother wrote a third time to the friary and Padre Pio. She was going to mail the letter on Christmas morning.

Meanwhile, around two a.m. on Christmas, Gianfranco sat up in bed and asked for something to drink. Other than bringing up some mucus, he was fine. His coughing also disappeared.

Gianfranco told his family that during his illness, he had seen the Infant Jesus on his dresser. Baby Jesus had assured him that he would get better.

Later, when the physician checked Gianfranco, he was giving a clean bill of health!

The Lord accepted Padre Pio's prayers and sufferings for Gianfranco. The giving stigmatist had once again touched the life of a child and given him back his health.

He loved and prayed for everyone. Padre Pio's prayers and work had no limitations. He gave of himself freely.

Padre Pio explained that God didn't always grant him the miracles that people needed or wanted. The mystic said, "On the other hand, when the Lord does not want to grant my requests, He makes me forget to pray for them, although I had the best and firmest intention to do so."[5]

Padre Pio often said to pray and trust in the wonderful ways of the Lord.

Although Padre Pio's prayers for others continued, his forced imprisonment was taking a toll on his health. He was thinner and his beard had grown a bit grayer. His forty-seventh birthday was upon him. He was ready to begin a more active ministry.

CHAPTER 8

By May 1934, Pio's ministry was moving back on track. That was not to say that people surrounding Padre Pio didn't make problems for him.   Problematic people and situations continued to be his companions.

Padre Pio had a deep and profound desire to bring everyone to God. He worked nonstop for this cause. People were entranced with his Mass and profoundly touched when they confessed to him in the Sacrament of Penance. The Mass and Confession were powerful tools of the Lord that Padre Pio used to reach his children.

Many times, Padre Pio entered the church and turn toward the congregation. He would have a pensive look on his face as he searched the crowd. It was at this point that the insightful stigmatist would look inside people's souls. He searched for people in need of his help.

At the recitation of the Mass, the stigmatist actually suffered the Passion of Jesus. During the observing and participation of the Mass, people didn't see the stigmatist's sufferings. He went on to say, "Everything that Jesus suffered in his Passion I suffer also, inadequately, as much as it is possible for a human being."[1]

The people crowding Our Lady of Grace church not only wanted to hear his Mass, but also wanted to watch the changed expressions on

Padre Pio's beautiful face during the liturgy. Once the church doors opened, the crowd made a mad rush toward the front of the altar.

Maria Winowska, who was Padre Pio's biographer stated:

> The Capuchin's face which a few moments before had seemed to me jovial and affable was transfigured...fear, joy, sorrow, agony or grief...Suddenly great tears welled from his eyes, and his shoulders, shaken with sobs...Between himself and Christ there was no distance.[2]

Padre Pio, through his prayers, placed all the suffering and pain of humanity in the chalice. During the Consecration of the Mass, the bread and wine are changed to the body and blood of Jesus. It also represents the last hours that Jesus spent on the cross. At that point of the Consecration, Padre Pio saw all the people that had requested his intercession.

After the Consecration, he experienced the bitter taste of the gall, thirst and abandonment of the Lord Jesus on the cross. The stigmatized priest remained on the altar, but continued to spiritually suffer the terrible pains of Calvary. Padre Pio also hung from the cross during part of the Mass just as Jesus had done during the Crucifixion. At Christ's Crucifixion, the cross was placed on its side so the nails could be inserted in His hands and feet. Likewise, the stigmatist's cross that he spiritually experienced was placed on its side to symbolize the suffering of Jesus.

Padre Pio stated that he died "Mystically at the Holy Communion."[3] The Heavenly Hosts would remove him from the cross and place the mystic in the arms of St. Francis.

During Mass, Padre Pio also wore the crown of thorns as he suffered spiritually. The thorns remained around his head at all times. Padre Pio felt that this was necessary to complete the sacrifice. Regarding the pain of Christ's Passion, the stigmatist said, "I do not desire the suffering for itself, no; but for the fruit it gives. It gives Glory to God and saves the brethren."[4]

Although the large crowds that came to Padre Pio's mass didn't physically see his spiritual sufferings on the altar, a few were made privy to those extraordinary phenomena.

Miss Morcaldi lived in San Giovanni Rotondo. She was going to marry, and asked her fiancée to visit Padre Pio. He attended his Mass. Shortly after, the young man became very pale.

Padre Pio saw the young man and said, "Thank God for what you have seen, and don't tell anyone. God's secrets should be kept hidden in your heart."

The young man agreed and answered, "I have seen you on the altar, crowned with thorns, first with a triple crown of thorns, and then with something like a bonnet of thorns."

Padre Pio responded, "Go home, thank God, and tell no one."

The young man told his fiancée about what he had seen. Miss Morcaldi went to see the stigmatist.

Padre Pio responded, "Do you have any doubt?" You are like St. Thomas.

Many years later, still curious, she went back to the wise priest. She asked Padre Pio if he wore the crown of thorns all through Mass.

The stigmatist responded, "You certainly want to know too much. Yes, before and after Mass, the crown that God has put on me is never taken off."[5]

Padre Pio grew up in a family environment where things were said in a direct manner. Family members didn't mince their words. This influenced Pade Pio as he grew up. Throughout his life, some people didn't accept the stigmatist's direct ways.

Examples of the priest's character showed up in the Sacrament of Reconciliation.

The Sacrament of Penance was another way to bring people to God. Padre Pio was powerful in reaching his children. He showed exceptional perception in confession. The stigmatist would put the people at ease. In the Sacrament of Reconciliation, he reminded the individuals of sins that had slipped their minds. People were astounded.

Padre Pio could look into the souls of individuals to see where they stood in God's grace. Many times, he yelled at people and asked them to get out of the confessional or church. The dutiful priest chose those means to impress on their souls the wrong path they were taking. He even refused to start or conclude confessions.

The individuals walked out of the confessional in a daze. Padre Pio worked on their conscience. He went through so much pain to have those people come back to confession. He offered his suffering to God to insure that the individuals turned away would come back for a good and true confession. Padre Pio continued to have mysterious high fevers, stomach and other health problems that he offered to God. It went on and on. The Lord accepted his sufferings for those needy souls.

The people turned away would come back and beg Padre Pio to hear their confession. He always did. The priest wanted the individuals to reflect and change within. More times than not, the people previously turned away became devotees of Padre Pio. In the end, most of them believed and changed their ways.

Laurino Costa was a doubter. He was the head cook at Padre Pio's Hospital, called Home of Relief of Suffering. For three years, he doubted Padre Pio's holiness. One day, Mr. Costa went to confession to Padre Pio. When he entered the confessional, he saw a deep cross on Padre Pio's forehead. The priest's face was covered with blood. Padre Pio didn't say anything to Mr. Costa.

Mr. Costa later said, "I began to tremble from fright. I called to him, but he didn't answer me. He just stared at me. And there was that cross, with blood flowing from it."

After some time Padre Pio came to and heard Mr. Costa's confession. When Mr. Costa came out of the confessional, he began to cry. Costa's emotional state continued for several days. Finally, he decided to confront Padre Pio, but began to cry upon seeing him.

Padre Pio asked him what was wrong.

Mr. Costa asked, "Padre, tell me, why did you make me see you like that? Is it perhaps I who make you suffer so?"

Padre Pio said, "What a dunce you are! It was a grace which God wanted to give you."[6]

Another example of Padre Pio's power of confession occurred when a Mr. Saltamerenda visited a friend on his way to Rome. His friend was a spiritual child of Padre Pio. Mr. Saltamerenda noticed a picture of Padre Pio at his friend's house. Shortly after, he felt a funny sensation in his throat. He continued to Rome. The next day, he heard a voice asking that he return to San Giovanni Rotondo. When Mr. Saltamerenda returned, the contraction in his throat continued several times. As he attempted to go to confession, Padre Pio asked him, "Tell me son, don't you ever think of your own miserable soul?"

Mr. Saltamerenda responded, "For the propagation of the species."

Padre Pio answered, "You wretch. Don't you see that your soul is being destroyed?"

He placed his hand on Mr. Saltamerenda's mouth and said, "Go."

Padre Pio's hands on his mouth made a deep impression on the gentleman. He wanted to go back and confess. He hid amongst a group of men.

Padre Pio yelled, "Genoese, you have a dirty face. You live near the sea, but you don't know how to wash. You are a big ship without a captain."

Mr. Saltamerenda tried to get near Padre Pio, but Padre Pio sent him away. He stumbled outside dazed. No matter where he went, Padre Pio worked on his conscience. When he returned to the church, another priest took him to Padre Pio's room. On the way to Padre Pio's room, Mr. Saltamerenda smelled a beautiful fragrance of violets.

Padre Pio grumbled, "What do you want? Don't make me waste my time. Go downstairs and I'll hear your confession."[7]

Padre Pio heard his confession and helped Mr. Saltamerenda recall all his sins. Later, in his room, Mr. Saltamerenda heard knocking on the doors, windows and walls. He was afraid. The gentleman prayed to Padre Pio for help. The noises stopped and the room was filled with wonderful fragrances.

The sweet aromas of a flower garden continued to flow into the hearts of people.

CHAPTER 9

On February 15, 1950, Dr. Duodo was talking to a group of friends. Shortly after, the group felt engulfed with a wonderful smell of violets. The aroma lasted for quite a while. Another physician present was a Dr. Bianco. He added that the fragrances were that of carnations, roses and violets. Dr. Duodo gave testimony to this incredible experience.

Many have felt that the delightful fragrances that so many people experienced came from the blood of the stigmata on Padre Pio's hands, feet, and side. The perfume that emanated from Padre Pio was also of lilies, incense and tobacco. People smelled these odors whenever God bestowed favors on them through the intercession of the humanitarian priest.

People who knew the ways of Padre Pio realized that the perfume or aroma was an indication that he had heard their prayers. They also understood that the aromatic fragrances could be a warning toward danger or to stop certain actions. The fragrances were Padre Pio's way of saying to pray, hope and have faith. Padre Pio's children felt his spiritual presence even if he wasn't there in a physical form. His followers knew not to worry because the priest had their interest at heart. Those who had not heard of the stigmatized priest soon learned of his ways.

Many people smelled Padre Pio's perfume before they went to see him. Other times, the fragrance came after individuals concluded their visit. Padre Pio's perfume could reach individuals while traveling in cars or trains, or simply walking. Many times, objects that he touched were blessed with his charismatic odor. Not even the distances between the oceans or seas, mountains or hills, countries or continents could stop his powerful intercessions.

While for others it would come as a wisp in the wind, the perfume odor always assured the closeness of Padre Pio's spirit.

In 1950, a seminarian served one of Padre Pio's masses. He wasn't aware of the many wonders of Padre Pio. He later told a priest that while reciting prayers at the foot of the altar, he smelled a wonderful perfume that was unknown to him. The priest smiled and explained to the young seminarian the gifts of the stigmatized Padre Pio. The priest told the seminarian that he had received an answer to his prayers through the intercession of Padre Pio.

In 1953, twenty-year-old Gianmaria came down with tonsillitis or a severe sore throat. His fever reached 104 degrees Fahrenheit. His father, a physician, gave his son various antibiotics, which didn't work. A friend of the family brought a statue of the Blessed Mother, a picture of Padre Pio and bottled water blessed by the stigmatist. The doctor gave his son spoonfuls of the blessed water until it was finished. Later, the young man's temperature not only came down, but the infectious tonsils were healed.

As Gianmaria came to, he whispered, "Because of this fresh and perfumed air I am coming back to life."[1]

The father had asked Padre Pio for his intercession. The family had continued to pray for the recovery of their young man.

A young girl became violently sick after her First Holy Communion. Vomiting, coughing and a temperature of 104 degrees accompanied her illness. A doctor was immediately called. Meanwhile, one of the guests suggested that the group pray to Padre Pio and the Blessed Mother. Shortly after, the little girl was better.

The young girl opened her eyes and said that she smelled sweet incense used in church.

The physician came to examine the little girl. He found that her temperature was close to normal. The doctor found only a mild form of bronchitis.

The chrisms of Padre Pio didn't stop with the stigmata. He continued to have the gift of prophecy, the gift of speaking other languages, healing the sick, and the ability to see into the souls of all the individuals that came into the confessional.

The stigmatized priest carried on with his work despite continued distractions.

CHAPTER 10

From the early 1920's to 1968, Padre Pio lived in the friary at San Giovanni Rotondo. He made an exception in May 1917 and accompanied his sister, Graziella, upon entering the convent of Our Lady of Sorrow in Rome. The stigmatist also left the monastery to pay his respect at the death of his mother and then his father's in 1946. After that, Padre Pio would leave the friary only to vote, to see the hospital he helped build, or make a few speeches pertaining to religious committees within his order.

Through his gift of bilocation, he continued traveling the world. The different forms of Padre Pio's bilocation were the power of vanishing and the ability to be seen.

Other times, individuals heard his voice clearly in different parts of the world. Often, his voice would come in their dreams to help and console.

Whatever form Padre Pio used through the greatness and kindness of God, people were helped with their needs.

In 1931 Padre Pio did a vanishing act. An actor came to San Giovanni Rotondo to meet and be converted by Padre Pio. The actor thought this was very amusing! He waited and waited, but Padre Pio was nowhere in sight. The people assured the actor that Padre Pio would arrive. When the gentleman got tired of waiting, he left.

Moments later, Padre Pio appeared to the astonished crowd waiting in the church.

They asked the priest of his whereabouts. Padre Pio replied, "I was right here, I passed in front of you three or four times, but neither you nor he noticed me."[1]

When Padre Pio had a few moments to relax, he often enjoyed sitting in the friary garden at San Giovanni Rotondo. The monastery garden was the only place he could be alone and pray his continuous rosary.

Even during those times, he was in transit. Padre Pio didn't like to talk about his bilocation experiences. From time to time, the other priests would obtain some information by sheer accident.

During a discussion time, one of the priests was wondering if the individuals going through the process of bilocation were aware of their movement. Padre Pio replied that the individuals knew what was going on.

On June 12, 1952, Lucia Bellodi, was dying with a form of diabetes. Her parents had taken her to many hospitals, but couldn't find any help for her health problem. On that day, Padre Pio came to Lucia (Lucy) in bilocation. Somehow, she misunderstood the message that Padre Pio gave her. She understood that her health wouldn't improve.

Due to her condition, Lucia's abdomen was deformed. Her only relief from unrelenting thirst was to drink water. Lucia was staying at a nursing home facility. She had asked the mother superior to take her to the chapel to pray. She declined any offer of water.

She prayed in the chapel, but feeling weak and faint was returned to her room. She was offered medical attention, but Lucia resisted any help.

While Lucia was in a slumber, Padre Pio had told her, "You are cured. Get up! Come immediately to my monastery."[2]

On June 17, 1952, Lucia went to see Padre Pio with the two nuns who had been with the young girl. Padre Pio blessed her and said, "I have been waiting for you."[3]

Prayer groups often were held at the homes of Padre Pio's spiritual children. One such meeting included a group of the Third Order of Saint Francis. The meeting place was at the home of Marshal Trombetta. The group prayed to the guardian angels to tell Padre Pio to be with them during the meeting. Many times, the group would smell the perfume of Padre Pio.

At one point during a meeting, Mr. Trombetta's five- year-old son Giovannino said, "Mamma, I am afraid, because Padre Pio is here. I see him."

Mrs. Trombetta asked her son where Padre Pio was. The boy pointed his finger and answered, "Now he is here, now he is there. He is still with us." Then Giovannino replied, "He is going away now."

When some of the members had asked Padre Pio if he had been at the meeting, he answered, "And who else could it have been?"[4]

Another time, Padre Pio gave further explanation of bilocation to his friend, Dr. Sanguinetti.

Dr. Sanguinetti asked the stigmatist, "When God sends a saint, for instances St. Anthony to another place by bilocations, is the saint aware of what is happening?"

Padre Pio responded, "One moment he is here, and the next moment he is where God wants him."

Dr. Sanguinetti, "But is he really in two places at once?"

"Yes," Padre Pio answered.

"How is this possible?"

"By a prolongation of his personality,"[5] Padre Pio explained.

The brightness of the light kept shining, while the enemies attempted to cast many shadows.

CHAPTER 11

As 1960's approached, Padre Pio continued to work for the betterment of humanity, yet he was becoming frail and was preparing to go to his heavenly home. God had other plans for His good priest.

In 1959, the stigmatist became ill and almost died. Doctors were called in. They diagnosed a tumor in the area of the lung. The doctors suggested chemotherapy. Padre Pio and his personal physician dismissed that finding. Both knew Padre Pio had pleurisy. Pleurisy is inflammation of the lining of the lungs.

The Conference of Italian Bishops wanted to ready the new decade. For this reason, they made 1959 a year of prayers. To honor that important year, the Conference of Italian Bishops had the statue of The Blessed Mother of Fatima visit the cities of Italy. In 1917, the Blessed Mother of Fatima had appeared to three peasant children in Portugal. The Virgin Mary had made many prophecies to these children.

When the Blessed Mother of Fatima came to San Giovanni Rotondo, Padre Pio was still sick. He was brought to The Blessed Lady in a wheelchair to pay his love and respect.

As the statue of The Blessed Mother was leaving for other destinations in Italy, Padre Pio watched from a window. He began to cry and said, "Madonna, my mother. You came to Italy and I was ill. Now you are going away and leaving me still sick"

Shortly after, the stigmatist felt a cold sensation go through his body. He then said, "I am cured."[1]

The Blessed Mother whom Padre Pio had loved with all his heart had heard his pleas.

News of his miracle from the Blessed Virgin spread throughout the world. Huge crowds from all over the world kept coming. Padre Pio returned to the business of his ministry.

Troubles and heartaches struck once again.

In the late 1950's, the Capuchin Orders made some bad investments decisions. They lost money. The Capuchins wanted Padre Pio to hand over the money from the hospital to pay their bills. Tremendous pressure was placed on Padre Pio, but he refused. Finding themselves in such dire strait, some administrators in the Capuchin Order even attempted to take the Home of Relief of Suffering away from him.

His enemies continued to belittle Padre Pio. They reported him to the Vatican.

The media also did their share of placing negative light on Padre Pio.

In 1960, Pope John XXIII, the newly elected pope, started an investigation of Padre Pio. The stigmatist was 73 years old. The news of the investigation came just before Padre Pio's fiftieth anniversary of his ordination into the priesthood!

Bad feelings flowed back and forth between the administrators of the hospital and members of the monastery at San Giovanni Rotondo.

They accused each other of taking money. Padre Pio was sad. He was instrumental in having the hospital built. The stigmatist didn't approve of this kind of behavior.

The Vatican sent Monsignor Carlo Maccari and his assistant, Father Giovanni Barberini to investigate. They investigated the running of the Home of Relief of Suffering, the ministry of Padre Pio and his private life. Representatives from the Vatican wanted to delve into the stigmatist's private ways. Some of Padre Pio's followers refused to talk to the people from Rome. The followers felt enough was enough.

Padre Pio was confused and bewildered by the investigation. He felt that his rights and freedom were going to be taken away, again. The stigmatist was correct.

Meanwhile, Padre Pio found out that his confessional and receiving room had been wiretapped in 1959. The priest was devastated. He shed many tears.

When the archbishop of the area found out that Padre Pio's confessional had been bugged, he went to see Padre Pio. As soon as the priest saw his archbishop, he ran to his arms saying that his own Capuchin brothers had been involved in the bugging of his confessional.

The controversy about the confessional still goes on to this day. The Capuchin Order has denied that the confessional was wiretapped, while others feel they have proof that it was bugged.

When Padre Pio's friends heard about how he was been treated, they came to his aide. Emmanuel Brunnato, an old protector of Padre Pio, sent a report to the United Nations for Human Rights. The Vatican, in its newspaper, denied that Padre Pio's confessional was wiretapped. Mr. Brunnato and friends made sure that the information of the wiretapped incident was reported in another paper.

The Vatican's representatives made a report and brought it to Rome. After the wiretapped incidents some members of the Capuchin Order were transferred from San Giovanni Rotondo.

In 1961, Cardinal Ottaviani read Monsignor Maccari's report on the investigation. Shortly after, Padre Pio had to adhere to the following rules: Bishops and priests couldn't serve Padre Pio's Mass, the Mass was to be at various times during the day, the followers could not talk to Padre Pio as he was going or coming back from confessional, people could not enter the church while the good priest was hearing confessions without tickets, Padre Pio was not allowed to talk to women in the receiving room or any other areas and railings were placed around the women's confessionals.

The hospital that Padre Pio had built would no longer be under his domain. On November 17, 1961, Father Clement Neubauer made a visit to Padre Pio. The Vatican wanted his hospital. Padre Pio signed over the Home for Relief of Suffering to the Holy See with complete obedience.

Padre Pio was again made a prisoner of the monastery.

Between 1960 and 1964, the stigmatist was often ill. He would become dizzy and at times fell down. When Padre Pio fell down, no one helped. Only a few of the friars were openly involved in these despicable acts.

When the media got hold of all that was done to Padre Pio, they questioned the Capuchin leaders. Uncomfortable with the media's attention, the superiors wanted Padre Pio to sign a document stating that the incidents weren't true. He refused.

Later, the Capuchin General went to see Cardinal Ottaviani in Rome. An arrangement was discussed. The new document would say that the restrictions were removed without any mentions of past incidents. This was supposed to be for the good of the Capuchin Order and the Catholic Church. In 1964, the document was presented to Padre Pio. He signed it.

The leaders of the Capuchin Order made attempts to have the information published in the Italian newspaper. They were refused. The media continued to have doubts that the restrictions had been lifted.

When newspaper reporters were able to see Padre Pio, the priest told them he was not free to come and go. He told the reporters the restrictions still continued.

However, on January 30, 1964, Cardinal Ottaviani allowed Padre Pio to resume his ministry. Padre Pio didn't have any bad feelings towards his enemies. In fact, he continued to show respect and present them in prayers to God.

But unfortunately, the end was nearing for Padre Pio.

CHAPTER 12

In 1965, Padre Pio went through a personal heartache. He received a visit from his sister, Suor Pia. She informed her brother that she had left the Brigittine Order in Rome after fifty years of service. Suor Pia had left due to internal dissension amongst the Order. The brother and sister spoke several times. Padre Pio wanted his sister to go back to the convent even though their actions were wrong. He believed in complete obedience to one's order. His sister refused. Unresolved issues remained. Sister Pia left her brother. They never spoke again.

Padre Pio became depressed. He prayed that she would return to her convent, but God did not answer his prayers. Padre Pio became distant and quiet. Many times the other priests heard Padre Pio say, "The Lord doesn't listen to my prayers anymore!"[1]

His health continued to deteriorate. He went on with his ministry the best he could. He used a wheelchair. Fellow priests were assigned to help him night and day. He felt as if he was imposing on his fellow priests. Many times, he cried when he couldn't do things for himself.

Padre Pio continued to say the rosary around-the-clock for the salvation of souls. Not once did he stop praying for the needs of his children throughout the world. His masses now lasted less than an hour. Padre Pio still heard about fifty confessions a day.

His stigmata had begun to disappear about a year earlier, especially from his feet. The wound at Padre Pio's side had also gone. In the summer of 1968, the wounds on his hands had disappeared. Many believed that this was an indication that his ministry and life were coming to a closing.

The Capuchin Order had been building a resting-place in a crypt under the new church for their gentle stigmatist. Padre Pio had prophesied that when his resting-place was completed, he would go to his heavenly home.

September 20, 1968 was the fiftieth anniversary of his visible stigmatization. Everyone celebrated. The church was decked out with roses from his spiritual children all over the world. Padre Pio said his usual mass in the early morning and proceeded with his usual routines. When people asked how he was feeling, he responded, "Only the cemetery remains."[2]

That night, his spiritual children continued the celebration by walking up to the monastery with candles. Padre Pio, exhausted by the day's events, slept.

September 22, 1968 began the First International Convention of Prayer Groups. At that time, 750 prayer groups all over the world had been established. Padre Pio was going to celebrate mass. He was happy that the Vatican had approved the prayer groups. He wanted the prayer groups in every country!

His spiritual children came from all walks of life. As soon as they saw him in the wheel chair, the crowd cheered and cheered. The priest sang the High Mass for that celebration. When the mass was concluded, the crowd of over four thousand shouted, "Long Live Padre Pio!"[3]

As Padre Pio got up from his chair behind the altar, he stumbled and almost fell. Other priests standing nearby caught him. As he was taken to the sacristy in the wheel chair, he called out, "My children. My children."[4]

He was not only weak but also looked very pale. Shortly after he was taken to his room, some of his relatives came to visit him. Later, he ate some lunch. He even went to the window to bless the enormous crowd below and wave with a handkerchief.

Even at the end of his life, the demons came to assault him. Padre Pio was terrified and begged his assistant, Padre Pellegrino, "Stay with me, my son."[5]

The early morning of the twenty-third, Padre Pio rose from bed with the help of Padre Pellegrino. He walked to the balcony and sat down for a few minutes. In coming back to his bed, Padre Pio fell in the chair. Padre Pellegrino alerted the others.

The priests rushed into the room. The doctors tried to revive the beloved stigmatist. He was given the Last Rites of the Catholic Church. Padre Pio was heard saying over and over, "Gesu, Maria, Gesu, Maria,"[6] (Jesus, Mary, Jesus, Mary).

Padre Pio went to his heavenly home on September 23, 1968 at 2:30 in the morning.

EPILOGUE

Canonization is the announcement of the Catholic Church that a deceased individual is written in the catalog of the saints. Only the Pope can issue the decree of canonization. A decree is a law or ruling. The decree states that the members of the Catholic Church may honor the individual canonized as a saint. The steps to canonization are many. It takes time and effort on the part of the Vatican to carefully study the life of an individual who will be appointed saint.

A canonization is granted only after a complete study of the candidate's life. The study must show that the candidate lived a pure and exemplary way of life.

After his beatification on May 2, 1999, the Vatican chose one significant miracle that occurred after the death of Padre Pio and through his intercession to the Lord. The miracles and favors, which he was able to give his beloved children through God's love, are many. Written testimonies from all over the world has been made available to the Vatican.

Jacob Hafer lives with his parents in Douglassville, Pennsylvania, not far from the Padre Pio Centre. In 1996, his parents took him for a check up, and the doctors found congenital malformation of the heart. Padre Pio was instrumental in Jacob's recovery.

The following is a letter from Jacob's mother regarding the grace that her son received from Padre Pio. Mrs. Hafer gave permission to the author to edit her letter:

Jacob was born on Valentine's Day, 1996, with a broken heart! He spent the first month of his life in the hospital. Over the course of three years, the doctors wanted to perform operations on Jacob's heart...We agreed to the surgeries, but were scared and sad that he would have to go through all the pain.

I didn't know about Padre Pio, yet. One day, I was very sad and called my mom. She told me to pray to Padre Pio...I began to pray. We took Jacob to the National Centre for Padre Pio in Barto, Pa. Jacob was not only blessed with Padre Pio's glove but also wrapped in his Shawl.

At two months of age, we took Jacob to Dr. Pierantonio Russo for a second opinion.

Although we were confused about our son's future, we continued to pray to Padre Pio. We sat down to talk with Dr. Russo at St. Christopher Hospital in Philadelphia, Pennsylvania. I asked him if he'd ever heard of Padre Pio. The doctor stated that when he was a child in Italy, he attended Padre Pio's mass every week until 1965. Dr. Russo's father had been on the

Planning Board for the stigmatist's hospital in Italy. The physician said that if there were pediatric heart surgeries for children, he'd be involved. At that moment, we knew who to entrust our son for a new heart.

By praying to Padre Pio, we were not only allowed to obtain a second opinion but give our son a quality life. Through Padre Pio, Dr. Russo did just that.

Jacob received his new heart on September 26, 1996. He was seven and half months.

We thank Padre Pio everyday in our prayers. Our prayers continue for the little five-year-old boy who died in a car accident and his family who donated his heart for Jacob. The little boy is in heaven, but his heart is still beating...in our son. Mrs. Hafer

The following is another example of Padre Pio's wondrous miracle. Mrs. Walsh and Paul gave the author permission to paraphrase the Paul Walsh's recovery story as written by Mrs. Walsh in the newsletter of "Spirit of St. Madeline's."

On December 2, 1983 seventeen year-old Paul Walsh was in a car accident. He had cranial and facial injuries. His left eye was cut, and most of the iris was lost during the accident. Five specialists worked on Paul during the ten hours of surgery. His situation remained critical. Cerebral-spinal fluid was leaking in the area of his skull. Paul went into a coma.

His parents were beside themselves. Devout Catholics, they invoked the help of many saints.

Finally, someone mentioned Padre Pio. The first time Mrs. Walsh prayed to the stigmatist, Paul's right hand slowly moved up from his side onto his forehead to make the Sign of the Cross.

Mr. and Mrs. Walsh contacted Mrs. Calandra of the Padre Pio Centre in Barto, Pennsylvania. A representative from the Centre went to the hospital with Padre Pio's glove. Paul was blessed with the glove. From that day on, Paul had not needed treatment for the Diabetes Insipidus, because the problem had disappeared.

Paul's condition still remained critical.

On March 21, 1983 Paul had a shunt operation to relieve the excessive fluid in his brain. A shunt is a procedure where a permanent drainage tube is placed in the area of the head.

Finally, the doctors told Paul's parents that he wouldn't recover and would remain in a vegetated state. Mrs. Walsh continued praying for her son. One night, she smelled a beautiful aroma. She later realized it was Padre Pio's perfume.

Meanwhile, Mrs. Calandra had visited the tomb of Padre Pio in San Giovanni Rotondo, Italy. She had touched Paul's picture to Padre Pio's tomb.

On Friday, April 6, 1984, Mr. Calandra again blessed Paul with Padre Pio's glove. Paul came out of the coma on April 7, 1984.

Good Friday of 1984, Paul received the final blessing with Padre Pio's glove.

On Easter Sunday, Paul told his parents that his Uncle Charley had visited him during the night. Paul's uncle lived out of state and couldn't have been there. When Mrs. Walsh showed her son a picture of Padre Pio, Paul responded, "That's exactly who visited me." His hospital roommate also verified that an old priest in a brown robe had entered the room in the early hours of Easter Sunday and blessed Paul. Paul later said that Padre Pio was instrumental in his recovery.

Shortly before being discharged from the hospital, Paul had surgery on his eyes. The doctor removed the cataract that had formed. On examination, the back of his damaged eye was perfectly healthy. Paul had perfect sight in one eye and was able to see from the injured one after he was fitted for a contact lens.

Paul Walsh gave written permission to the author to edit his letter regarding the miracle.

The following letter from Paul describes his life after Padre Pio's miracle.

Since the miracle, I have become so much more of a caring person. Everyday, I thank God for being alive and well. I enjoy going to church, regularly. I pray more often and feel much closer to God.

I work as a counselor with the mentally and physically disadvantaged. I feel that I must work at helping those less fortunate. The miracle has changed my focus on life to be more centered on God, and helping others with what I can. Perhaps, it's God plan for me to work with the disadvantaged and relate my cure. Today, I feel great. Paul Walsh

On December 18, 1997, Pope John II pronounced the Servant of God, Padre Pio of Pietrelcina "Venerable." This was an important step toward his canonization. It was also the official closing of the beatification process. Pope John II and the Cardinals have approved and signed all the necessary documents.

The next step was to have the Vatican accept a miracle through the intercession of Padre Pio since his death on September 23, 1968. The investigation of this miracle has been approved. There was a beatification ceremony at the Basilica of St. Peter in Rome. Millions of people attended the ceremony. This long awaited day was on May 2, 1999. From that time, The Venerable Padre Pio has been called Blessed. This was an important step toward his eventual sainthood.

After three years of continued study, Pope John II approved the canonization of Blessed Padre Pio. On June 16, 2002, the Pope proclaimed Blessed Padre Pio of Pietrelcina a Saint. From that moment on, his new name was Saint Pio of Pietrelcina. The canonization ceremony was held in Saint Peter's Square in Rome, Italy.

The Prayer Groups that the Saint Pio began are presently in the thousands. In Italy alone, the prayer groups exceed 2,000. Over 1,000 Prayer Groups are in existence through out the rest of the world.

Saint Pio of Pietrelcina died on September 23, 1968. Saint Pio remains the only stigmatized priest in the history of the Catholic Church. Thousands of people from all over still come to pay their respect for this holy man. He is buried in his resting-place, beneath the sanctuary of Our Lady of Grace Friary church, in San Giovanni Rotondo, Italy.

Elvira Mucciarone Janz

FOOTNOTES

Chapter 1

1. Vera Calandra, personal interview, 1997.

2. Alessio Parente, O.F.M. Capuchin, *"Send Me Your Guardian Angel" Padre Pio* (Italy, 1987) p 19.

3. Da Alessandro Ripabottoni, Capuchin, *Pio of Pietrelcina - Infancy and Adolescence* (Italy, 1969) p 50.

4. Calandra, Interview.

5. Padre Pio, Capuchin, Personal letter to his father, *Voice of Padre Pio, Vol. 11 Number - 4* (Italy, 1972), From University of Dayton-Marianist Library.

6. John A. Schug, O.F.M. Capuchin, *Padre Pio* (Barto, PA 1995) p 28.

7. Calandra, Interview.

8. Schug, p 29.

9. Schug, p 30.

10. Augustine McGregor, O.C.S.O. *Padre Pio-His Early Years*, Edited by Father Gerard Di Flumeri (Italy, 1981) p 96.

Chapter 2

1. Bernardino of Siena, "The Church - The Blessed Mother," *Padre Pio of Pietrelcina, Spirituality Series-1 Acts of the First Congress of Studies on Padre Pio's Spirituality*, (Italy, 1972) p 159.

2. Vera Marie Calandra, Phone Interview, 1998.

Chapter 3

1. Augustine McGregor, O.C.S.O., *Padre Pio's Early Years* (Italy, 1981) p 134 - 135.

2. Fernando of Riese Pio X, "The Mystery of the Cross in Padre Pio," *Padre Pio of Pietrelcina Spirituality Series-1 Acts of the First Congress of Studies On Padre Pio's Spirituality,* San Giovanni Rotondo, May 1-6, 1972 (Italy, 1972). p 96.

3. Padre Pio of Pietrelcina, Letters Vol.1, Editions "Padre Pio da Pietrelcina" (Italy, 1984) p 271.

4. Padre Pio of Pietrelcina, Letters Vol.1, Editions "Padre Pio da Pietrelcina" (Italy, 1984) p 311.

5. Elvira M. Janz, "Guardian Angels All Around," *Echoes of Padre Pio's Voice* (Barto, Pa. 1998) p 8.

6. Janz, p 8.

Chapter 4

1. Schug, p 69.
2. Schug, p 74.
3. Bernardino of Siene, *Padre Pio of Pietrelcina Spirituality Series - 1, Acts of the First Congress of Studies On Padre Pio's Spirituality, San Giovanni Rotondo, May 1 - 6, 1972,* "Padre Pio The Church—The Blessed Mother." p 155.
4. Addolorata Taddeo Mucciarone, Personal Interview, 1997.

Chapter 5

1. Dorothy M. Gaudiose, *Prophet Of The People, Biography of Padre Pio* (Staten Island, New York, 1974) p 87.

2. Schug, p104.

3. Schug, p 104.

4. Schug, p 105-106

Chapter 6

1. Settimio Cipriani, *Padre Pio of Pietrelcina Spirituality Series - 1, Acts of the First Congress of Studies On Padre Pio's Spirituality, San Giovanni Rotondo, May 1 - 6, 1972,* "The Search for God." Edited by Gerardo Di Flumeri, O.F.M., (Italy, 1972) p 57.

2. Gaudiose, p 91.

3. John A. Schug, O.F.M., Capuchin, *A Padre Pio Profile,* (Massachusetts, 1987) p 57.

Chapter 7

1. John A. Schug, O.F.M., Capuchin, *Padre Pio* (Barto, Pa, 1995) p 101.

2. Calandra, Interview.

3. Charles Mortimer Carty, Reverend, *Padre Pio The Stigmatist* (Rockford, Illinois, 1973) p 177.

4. Carty, p 158.

5. Schug, p 134.

Chapter 8

1. Father Tarcisio of Cervinara, *Padre Pio's Mass,* (Italy, 1992) p 24.
2. John A. Schug, Capuchin, *Padre Pio,* (Pa. 1995) p 109-110.
3. Tarcisio, p 53.
4. Tarcisio, p28.
5. Schug, p 113.
6. Schug p 114, 116.
7. Carty, p 128-129.

Chapter 9

1. Clarice Bruno, *Roads To Padre Pio,* (Pa. 1981) p 133.

Chapter 10

1. Reverend Charles Mortimer Carty, *Padre Pio The Stigmatist*, (Illinois, 1989) p 61.
2. Carty, p 170.
3. Carty, p 170.
4. Carty, p 62-63.
5. Carty, p 69.

Chapter 11

1. Bernardino of Siena, "The Church - The Blessed Mother," *Padre Pio of Pietrelcina, Spirituality Series-1 Acts of the First Congress of Studies on Padre Pio's Spirituality*, (Italy, 1972) p 165.

Chapter 12

1. Interview, 1997.
2. Calandra, Interview, 1997.
3. Calandra, Interview, 1997.
4. Gaudiose, 234.
5. Gaudiose, 235.
6. Bruno, 229.

BIBLIOGRAPHY

Acts Of The First Congress Of Studies On Padre Pio's Spirituality,
Padre Pio of Pietrelcina Spirituality Series-1, May 1-6, 1972,
Edited by Gerardo Di Flumeri, O.F.M., Capuchin (San Giovanni
Rotondo, Italy, 1972).

Allegri, di Renzo, *Messaggero di Santo Antonio*, "Il Tocco Della
Grazia," p.26-27 (Padua, Italy, 1998).

Bernardino of Siena, *The Church - The Blessed Mother*, Padre Pio of
Pietrelcina, Spirituality Series-1 Acts of the First Congress of
Studies on Padre Pio's Spirituality, (Italy, 1972).

Bruno, Clarice, *Roads To Padre Pio*, National Centre For Padre Pio
(Barto, Pa., 1981).

Calandra, Vera M. Personal Interview. 29 July 1997.

Calandra, Vera M., Audiotape, "Maria, The star who guides us to
Jesus," National Centre for Padre Pio, Inc. (Barto, Pa.).

Calandra, Veramarie, Oral Communication by phone, 19 Oct. 1998.

Carty, Charles Mortimer, Rev., *Padre Pio The Stigmatist,* Tan Publishers, Inc. (Rockford, Illinois, 1973).

Cipriani, Settimio, *The Search for God,* Padre Pio of Pietrelcina Series - 1, Acts of the First Congress of Studies On Padre Pio's Spirituality, (Italy, 1972).

Fernando of Riese Pio X, *The Mystery of the Cross in Padre Pio,* Padre Pio of Pietrelcina Spirituality Series -1 Acts of the First Congress of Studies on Padre Pio's Spirituality, (Italy, 1972).

Gaudiose, Dorothy M., *Prophet Of The People,* National Centre For Padre Pio (Barto, Pa. 1992).

Hafer, Kathy, Written Communication, 5 Nov. 1998; 6 April 1999.

Hafer, Kathy, Oral Communication by phone, 6 Feb. 1999; 6 April 1999.

Janz, Brian A. N.; M. D. Many hours of medical explanation; 1997-2001.

Janz, Elvira M., *Echoes of Padre Pio's Voice,* "Guardian Angels All Around," National Centre for Padre Pio, Inc. p.8 (Barto, Pa., 1998).

Janz, Elvira M., Written Communication to Mr. Paul Walsh, 11 Oct. 1998.

Janz, Elvira M., Written Communication to Mrs. Kathy Hafer, 11 Oct. 1998.

Maria Di Santa, di Valentino, *Voce Di Padre Pio*, "La vita mistica di Padre Pio," 2, p. 5, 6, 8, Edizione "Padre Pio" (San Giovanni, Rotondo, 1978).

McGregor, Father Augustine, O.C.S.O., *Padre Pio His Early Years*, Editions "Padre Pio da Pietrelcina (San Giovanni Rotondo, Italy, 1981).

Mucciarone, Addolorata Taddeo, Personal Interview, 1997.

Parente, Alessio, O.F.M., Capuchin, *"Send Me Your Guardian Angel"* (Italy, 1987).

Padre Pio of Pietrelcina, Letters Vol. I, Editions "Padre Pio da Pietrelcina" (Italy, 1984).

Padre Pio of Pietrelcina, Letters Vol. II, Editions "Padre Pio da Pietrelcina" (Italy, 1997).

Padre Pio of Pietrelcina, Letters Vol. III, National Centre for Padre Pio, Inc. (Barto, Pa., 1994).

Padre Pio, *The Voice of Padre Pio,* "Some Letters Of The Young Padre Pio" (San Giovanni Rotondo, 1972).

Ripabottoni, Alessandro Da, Capuchin, *Pio of Pietrelcina- Infancy and Adolescence*, Edizioni, Padre Pio da Pietrelcina (San Giovanni Rotondo, Italy, 1969).

Schug, John A., O.F.M., Capuchin, *Padre Pio*, National Centre for Padre Pio, Inc. (Barto, Pa., 1995).

Schug, John A. O.F.M., Capuchin, *A Padre Pio Profile,* St. Bede's Publication (Petersham, Massachusetts, 1987).

Tarcisio, Father, Of Cervinara, *Padre Pio's Mass*, Edited by Alessio Parente, O.F.M. Capuchin, *"Padre Pio da Pietrelcina"* Editions (Italy, 1992).

Walsh, Betty, Written Communication, 23 Oct. 1998; 8 April 1999.

Walsh, Paul, Written Communication, 23 Oct. 1998; 8 April 1999.

Walsh, Betty, Oral Communication, 24 March 1999.

Walsh, Paul, Oral Communication, 24 March 1999.

Walsh, Betty, *The Spirit of St. Madeline's,* "A Miracle in Our Midst,"
Vol. 4, No.11, (Pa. 1984).

White, Laura Chanler- Translation by, *Who Is Padre Pio?* Tan Books
and Publishers, Inc. (Rockford, Illinois, 1974).

ABOUT THE AUTHOR

Elvira Mucciarone Janz was born in Italy. Her family lived about three hours from St. Pio and San Giovanni Rotondo. At the age of nine, she moved to the United States with her family. The author grew up with the knowledge of St. Pio. She learned about St. Pio at an early age from her mother and grandmother who attended his masses.

Elvira Mucciarone Janz has a degree in Social Psychology. She graduated from Lake Erie College in Painesville, Ohio. She has a teaching certificate from the State of Ohio. The author is also an artist. She has worked with abstract art and portraits. Her work has appeared in many art shows. The author's abstract painting made the first judging in the Cleveland Museum Art May Show. She also worked on a mural in Cleveland, Ohio with Ed Glynn and other artists. Elvira Janz is married and has three children, Eric, Brian and Carla. In her free time, she enjoys reading, walking, and is a member of World Society Protection of Animals, Puppy Mill Fighters, and PETA. She not only writes about the plight of abused and slaughtered animals, but also is an animal rescuer. The author loves taking care of her bichon frises.

The author's research took many twists and turns. She first informally interviewed family and friends about St. Pio, read and researched books, articles, documentaries, made trips to various areas of the United States and was in touch with the monastery in San Giovanni Rotondo, Italy. Father Gerardo Di Flumeri, Vice Postulator in San Giovanni Rotondo gave the author permission to use St. Pio's pictures, to properly quote his words and paraphrase freely from any books published by *Editions Padre Pio of Pietrelcina* or from *Voice of Padre Pio*. Father Gerardo Di Flumeri requested that a copy of the author's book be sent for the archives at San Giovanni Rotondo, Italy. Father Gerardo Di Flumeri wrote a moving statement about St. Pio for the author's book.

During this time, the author also wrote an article called "Guardian Angels All Around." It was published in the *Echoes of Padre Pio's Voice*.

While writing and researching her book, the author received a letter of encouragement from Pope John II. The encouragement was very much appreciated.

The author interviewed Mrs. Vera Calandra and Veramarie Calandra from the National Centre for Padre Pio in Barto, Pennsylvania. Veramarie had received a lifesaving miracle from St. Pio when she was a young child. Mrs. Hafer was interviewed regarding the miracle her son Jacob had received. Also interviewed was Mrs. Walsh. Paul Walsh had received a miracle from St. Pio after a near fatal car accident.

Elvira Mucciarone Janz continues writing short articles. She has begun working on a second book.

Printed in the United States
879200004BB